The **Father**...
The **Son**...
and the
Sweet Sixteen

A COLLEGE'S BASKETBALL DISASTER

PAUL WIELAND

ISBN: 0615478123
ISBN-13: 9780615478128
Library of Congress Control Number: 2011906125
Brown Hill, Great Valley, NY

Chapter One

Bob Wickenheiser once was a rainmaker. When he walked into a job, he took on challenges head-on and used his intelligence, management skills and driving personality to get things done his way.

Or he sent his subordinates onto the highway.

Wickenheiser comes from tough North Dakota stock, one of the German Catholics who with German Lutherans made up much of the early population of the state. He is tall, with close-cropped hair, military in appearance. Put him into a uniform and he could easily pass for a commanding general.

He learned how to command by being commanded, spending four years as a Benedictine monk in North Dakota, where he attended St. Benedict's College. The Benedictines aren't considered the strictest of the Roman Catholic Church's monastic orders, but being a Benedictine monk is hardly a walk in the park.

Being a Benedictine requires obedience to authority, namely to the monk in charge of the monastery, and, of course, to the rules of the order, as well as the basic vows of poverty, chastity and obedience. Many monks are priests, but not all. It turned out that Bob Wickenheiser found another way to move forward in life, leaving the monastery, and deciding to pursue a master's and then a doctoral degree at the University of Minnesota. The degrees were in English literature, and Wickenheiser was an outstanding scholar. He was particularly interested in the English poet John Milton, an interest that eventually led him to be considered one of the world's leading Milton scholars.

His work snagged him appointment as an English professor at Princeton University where he taught until he was but 34 years old. Then he became one of the youngest college presidents in the history of Catholic education in the United States, signing on as the boss at Mount St. Mary's College in Emmitsburg, Md. The story could have ended here except for one thing: Bob Wickenheiser's passion for basketball.

Mount St. Mary's is now a university and proudly points out that it's on the list of the "10 most Catholic colleges" in the United States. This is how it identifies itself on its web site: "The Mount, founded in 1808 is the nation's second-oldest Catholic university and offers a rigorous educational experience rooted in the liberal arts that provide students with depth, substance and success. With 1,600 undergraduate students and a 13:1 student/faculty ratio, the Mount ensures an uncommon sense of community."

When Wickenheiser arrived Mount St. Mary's was struggling with finances. Its endowment was a measly $1-million, a number so low that it is shocking. When he left 16 years later, Wickenheiser had boosted the number to $15-million, and left a trail of controversies in his wake.

His academic aims conflicted with the traditional ones at the Mount. In his last year as president, Wickenheiser placed heavy emphasis on the school's education and business programs rather than its traditional liberal arts offerings. One of the college's most popular deans was replaced and there were student demonstrations against the change.

Since college and university life is much more rigid than one would think, every president who tries to make changes in the structure of a school faces resistance from some faculty and often from students. It comes with the territory. So Bob Wickenheiser was no different than any college president who wants changes and effects them.

But he also couldn't keep his hands off college basketball, even then, at the home of one of most successful coaches in U.S. college basketball history.

Wickenheiser's foray into the basketball program at Mount St. Mary's began with a letter he sent to the coach, Jack Phelan, six days before formal team practice began in the fall of 1992. Phelan was entering his 40th year of coaching the Mount. He had led teams to 14 NCAA tournaments, including a College Division Championship in 1982. The Mount had competed for many years at the what's now considered Division Two by the NCAA.

Phelan opened the president's letter to find Bob wanted him to retire at season's end instead of continuing his coaching career. Phelan is a Philadelphia Irishman, which gives him the cultural background to be just as stubborn as a North Dakota German. He was entering the 92-93 season seven wins short of the 700 mark, a feat that placed him in the stratosphere of US college basketball coaches. But Phelan's teams had been lousy for the previous two seasons, and Wickenheiser decided he wanted to pull the plug on his school's legendary coach.

Phelan was 63 in 1992, operating under a contract signed four years before that give him full salary every year to age 70, whenever—or if ever—he retired. The problem was that Phelan had no inclination to retire. His team was in the low-wattage Division One Northeast Conference with such national basketball powers as Wagner and Central Connecticut State. That's a cynical way to say his teams didn't play on a big stage, yet Phelan had made the most of what he could recruit for 39 years. His teams were always well drilled in fundamentals and hustled their way to wins they never should have posted.

Phelan made the letter from Wickenheiser public and that's when the court of public opinion leaned hard on the president. Hard enough, in fact, that he backed down immediately. "It was just a misunderstanding, and it has been straightened out," Phelan told the Baltimore Sun: "I don't expect this to come up now or later. For some reason, somebody must think I don't know when enough is enough. I will know when that time comes."

Wickenheiser was quoted as saying: "I don't want to get in a power struggle with Jim. If he wants to stay, he can stay. Most of all I want to see him get his 700 career wins." Wickenheiser actually had the whip hand, as he could have forced Phelan to retire under the terms of the contract. But he backed off in the face of a university community and alumni stacked against him.

The 92-93 season wasn't "that time," as Phelan's team went 13-15 and passed the 700 win mark for its coach. He was named the conference's co-coach of the year. Ironically, he was honored on the very day that Wickenheiser announced his resignation as he college's president.

Phelan hung on another decade at Mount St. Mary's, becoming the fourth coach in NCAA history to pass the 800-win plateau. He was inducted into the Basketball Hall of Fame in 2008.

Wickenheiser left the school with credit for pulling it through difficult financial times, and a bit of a black eye for trying to manipulate the basketball "program;" for trying to dump Phelan after two poor seasons. On May 10, 1993, Wickenheiser quit, saying he had no job in line. With four children, he needed to work. He could have returned to teach at Princeton, but St. Bonaventure beckoned, another school with dollar problems, and a great place to be a president if you loved college basketball. For college basketball was considered the life's blood of the Bonaventure image, a legacy of the Stith brothers and Bob Lanier; a place where basketball mattered more than just about anything else that happened on campus.

Chapter Two

There are crimson red tiles on most of the rooftops, emblematic of the Italian origins of the university, the roots of the man in whose name an order of religious was founded in the 15th century. Francis Of Assisi is known as the patron saint and protector of animals, subject of garden statues, a brown-robed, bearded symbol of peace and gentleness, hardly the model for deceit and ego-driven betrayal.

Four hundred years after Francis lived, priests in his Order of Friars came to Western New York with missionary zeal. These men were determined to bring the Franciscan way to Catholics and others who would feel the spirit of the brown robes; a spirit that has made even heathen understand Saint Francis cared about all God's creatures; fawns and foxes, squirrel and skunks, bluebirds, and even…basketball players.

I wish this was a cautionary tale, and I suppose in some ways it will be. But nothing seems to have changed for the better in the world of college sports, where caution is thrown into the winds of greed and avarice as regularly as coaches change their jobs.

This is a story about not long ago, but its roots lie in a different time- a more innocent time—when St. Bonaventure University first flexed its basketball muscle, and found it was addicted to the steroidal rush.

St. Bonaventure was 150 years old in 2008. The tiny liberal arts university tucked into a flat space among the hump hills of the Allegheny Mountains near the Alleghany River (Yes, there are two different spellings) had little to celebrate. That's because its falling enrollment left the university teetering on the edge of insolvency, even borrowing from its own endowment to balance the budget late in the same decade. Much of the problem went back to 2003, when the university's soul was scarred and its heart attacked by a scandal unique in the history of college athletics.

But first a look back to how it was possible that the university's soul went south, and many of its alumni hearts were broken.

After World War II college basketball was to begin its evolution into what it has become today—big business. That couldn't happen until college presidents, college trustees, state legislatures and ultimately—the United States Supreme Court—stepped forward to allow black Americans and black athletes to get an equal chance to play for any school they chose, and chose them.

Those first years after the war saw hesitant moves to equality—at least on the basketball court. Bill Russell starred at the San Francisco University, (a small Catholic school) and the first exceptional black ballplayer to step onto a national stage. In 1950, the City College of New York boasted a national championship team made up predominantly of black players.

Russell and CCNY were the first big win for black players, but the costs were equally devastating. Members of the CCNY team were implicated in a points-shaving scandal and their title taken away. Their disgrace on the national stage was the doom of major college ball at CCNY and nearly destroyed the lives of the point shavers.

It wasn't only the players at CCNY who played too fast and too loose. At the University of Kentucky, Coach Adolph Rupp proudly presented all-white rosters every season, as the defiant yahoo coach not only wouldn't recruit black players, he wouldn't schedule games against schools with black players on their rosters. Regardless, Kentucky was often the national champion, always one of the top-ranked teams in the country.

Coach Rupp's name is revered in Kentucky. The two seasons prior to CCNY's national title, Kentucky had been the national champion. Two of the Wildcats' stars— Alex Groza and Ralph Beard– were All-Americans and played on the 1948 Olympic gold medal United States team.

Their basketball careers also came to a sudden halt when the CCNY players were caught in a sting operation headed by New York District Attorney Frank Hogan. More than CCNY players were involved. There were 33 in all, including Groza and Beard. The points shaving tainted Manhattan College, New York University, Long Island University, Bradley and the University of Toledo.

Basketball coaches like to talk about "the program," referring to the regimen and structure of their team from recruiting through practices, lifestyle, and games. Division One basketball players are almost always on athletic scholarships. For most of these players that word is the closest they'll ever come to scholarly activity. The "program" at each of these colleges produced young men who compromised their integrity for a few bucks while shaving points in games.

That term—points shaving—refers to controlling the final score, the margin of victory. Let's say State U. is playing State A & M and State U. is a 12-point favorite. If anyone gambling knew that State U. wasn't going to cover that 12-point spread, that it was literally a sure bet, thousands could be made in a 40-minute game.

Gamblers who knew they had a sure bet had that knowledge because they bribed one or two players on State U. to make sure the final score resulted in a U. win by less than 12 points. Miss a jump shot here or there, miss foul shots, throw a bad pass, and State A&M lost by eight or nine points.

It didn't call for throwing a game, just controlling the final result. The gamblers made their thousands and those they bribed, a few hundred, if they were lucky. Contemporary sports journalists, as well as a few district attorneys, felt points shaving was a direct result of the game making it in the Big Apple, Madison Square Garden in New York.

After World War Two, the owners of the Garden scheduled weekend college basketball doubleheaders during the season, and invited teams from across the country to play against local powers such as CCNY, New York University, Long Island University, St. Johns and Manhattan. The Garden also promoted its own National Invitation Tournament in March, bringing together the best of the best college teams at season's end. The NIT was considered more prestigious than the NCAA tournament in those post-war years.

Getting a Garden date—a bite of the Big Apple—was a tempting thought for schools from coast to coast. Before the days of ESPN and March Madness, now with thousands of basketball games on television each season, there was only one way for a small school from the outlands to be known nationally, and that way was playing in the Garden at least once a year.

The Garden's eminence as a college basketball mecca rubbed off on other basketball venues. Four hundred miles upstate lay Buffalo's Memorial Auditorium, opened at the onset of World War II. The slate gray arena was a WPA project built during the worst years of the Depression, and held about 12,000 spectators for basketball. To fill those seats after the war, a local Jesuit college began serving as the basketball promoter.

Canisius College teams are known as the Golden Griffins, and were supported after the war by an alumni base that was almost entirely local. Postwar Canisius was a day-hop school, with no dormitories, and few places for students to live near the campus. When they graduated, Canisius alumni didn't leave town. They lived there. Thus a solid fan base existed.

Still, there weren't enough Canisius fans to fill those 12,000 Aud seats, and that's where St. Bonaventure, Niagara University and the national powers traveling to and from Madison Square Garden came into play.

First there was Niagara, another small Catholic liberal arts school operated by the Vincentian Fathers, situated on MontEagle Ridge, about 25 miles north of Buffalo in suburban Niagara Falls. Its teams are called the Purple Eagles, and to this day regularly appear in post-season tournaments, maintaining a tradition of excellence that began in the same years the scandal involving CCNY and Kentucky made headlines. Niagara and Canisius both had played CCNY in the season before the fixing was discovered, and both had won.

There was no evidence CCNY players had shaved points against Canisius or Niagara, but it's easy to assume just about anything could have happened. Despite the explosion of cheating in college basketball, there were never any accusations involving schools from Western New York. Canisius, Niagara and St. Bonaventure were known to their fans as the "Little Three." The title was a convenience as well as it was a rivalry, not a conference or formal structure. Each of the teams played the others twice a season, home and away. At least that was the theory, <u>except</u> the Aud basketball program run by Canisius changed that.

This was a big exception if one was a Niagara or Bonaventure fan. Canisius never played the others in anyplace but Memorial Auditorium, the Griffins home court.

It was probably a good idea for fans of college hoops. Bonaventure played its games in a stone barn three miles from campus in Olean, New York. The school's home court was a working National Guard armory, so only 1200 bleacher seats were available. We'll see more about the Olean Armory and its place in college basketball lore later on.

Niagara had a small gym on campus that had even more limited seating. Canisius had the big building to fill due to a contract with the City of Buffalo giving the college exclusive rights to Saturday nights. The college realized putting on attractive college basketball events would make it some money and raise its profile, so it began offering those Saturday night dates to teams traveling to and from the Garden in New York.

While Canisius had some fine teams shortly after the war and through the late 1950s, the basketball profiles of Bonaventure, and particularly, Niagara, were higher. The athletic department at Canisius solved the problem of opponents for teams passing through by scheduling doubleheader basketball every Saturday night in the winter. The first game featured Bo-naventure or Niagara against a team passing through, or twice a season against each other. The Griffs would always play the second game, with op-ponents drawn from the northeast, the traveling teams, or against Niagara or Bonaventure.

It wasn't unusual to see three of four teams on the doubleheader bill ranked in the nation's top 20. Nearly every renowned college basketball player in the nation played at least once in the Buffalo arena in his career.

These were the days when small Catholic schools such as those that made up the Little Three could gain national ranking and prominence quickly and easily.

There were several factors contributing to this. First, there were few con-ferences in college basketball, compared to today's landscape. The Big Ten was around, along with the Atlantic Coast, the SEC and the Pacific Coast. However, many of the best college basketball was being played by small independent programs such as LaSalle, Manhattan, Providence, Loyola of Chicago, Seattle, St. Francis of Pennsylvania, Fordham and Holy Cross.

Every one of the schools just named was a Catholic small college or university. Every one of those schools either had eliminated or downsized football because of the cost or would soon do so. These kinds of schools (including the Little Three) staked their athletic visibility on basketball.

How did they compete for players against the major conference institu-tions? That brings us to the second factor. It was as clear as black and white. These small Catholic schools admitted black basketball players. The major conference schools didn't. The ascendancy of black basketball players as the best in the game began in small Catholic colleges, and a few independents as well as in low tuition public institutions such as CCNY, the City College of New York.

Black Americans may have had civil rights after World War II, but exercis-ing those civil rights was a different matter. Baseball's Jackie Robinson, who broke the color line in major league baseball, first played for the Brooklyn Dodgers in 1947. In sports, as in the rest of American life, being black was a barrier to success. Those Catholic colleges with major college basketball programs were not just in it for the money or the notoriety that comes with winning an NIT or NCAA title. Oh, sure; the coaches knew they had an un-tapped well of talent in the first contingents of black basketball players. And they were the only ones drawing from the well.

Nevertheless, Catholic colleges in the northeast and the mid-west acted ethically on the basis of their religious foundations, giving black athletes a chance to get a college degree in exchange for their service as varsity athletes. It wasn't as easy as it seems. At. St. Bonaventure the first black play-ers arrived in the mid-50's and because they were but a tiny minority on the 800-student campus, there were white students who derided the basketball players on basis of their color alone.

Sam Stith was a Brooklyn kid who had played at St. Francis Prep there, and enrolled at Bonaventure in the fall of 1956. Stith was the first black high-profile recruit to Coach Eddie Donovan's team. Basketball player or not, Stith had to undergo two months of hazing and verbal abuse, the fortune of ev-ery freshman at the school. It must have been a rude shock to the Brooklyn kid who – after all—was a city boy on a rural campus where once students led a cow from an adjacent pasture to the third floor of a dormitory. Inciden-tally, cows don't much mind going up stairs, but will not go down them. The whole notion of hazing and freshman rules was based on building a team concept among the entire freshman class, and at St. Bonaventure it usually worked.

Stith was to be followed by his younger brother Tom, and another St. Francis Prep player, 6-4 Freddie Crawford. They would be the core of a St. Bonaventure team that was nationally prominent for five years run-ning. Today, not one of these black players would likely have ended up at St. Bonaventure. They were among the cream of the crop in recruits, and each made one All-American team or another during his career, as well as becoming a first-round NBA draft choice.

At tiny St. Bonaventure in the mid-50s, black athletes raised what had been a solid basketball "program" to national attention. It was the same thing at Niagara, though even sooner. The Niagara team included black stars Ed Fleming, Charlie Hoxie, and a terrific sixth man, rail-thin Tom Hemans. Fleming and Hoxie both went on to pro basketball careers after their graduation in 1955.

Canisius didn't have black players during the decade, but shared a com-mon situation with its Little Three opponents. They all had a coach, one coach…

At St. Bonaventure, the coach moved up from the job at nearby Olean High School. Eddie Donovan wasn't a local from Olean, but had settled there after graduation from St. Bona himself. He had no full-time assistant, though ex-Bona star guard Bob Sassone served as a part-timer.

At Niagara, John "Taps" Gallagher was the coach. Again…the only coach. Taps was a raconteur, one of the best after-dinner speakers a sports fan could find. And every time he unwound his Irish personality following a banquet meal, Gallagher not only sold Niagara basketball, he sold Niagara

University. His teams won at a .614 career rate and went to seven NIT tournaments when that was the mark of excellence.

Canisius was coached by Joe Curran from 1953 forward. His teams were most successful on the national stage in the mid-50's with back-to-back appearances in the NCAA tournament, and dominance of the Little Three. Curran worked alone as the Griffs coach, and succeeded without black players. Canisius began recruiting black players later than Bona and Niagara, but they would be instrumental in the school's success as years went by.

During a 10-year period beginning in the mid-50s it can be argued that there was no better place for quality college basketball in the country than the Little Three. There were All-Americans, high rankings, tournament teams, sell-out crowds in Buffalo's Memorial Auditorium, and in 1961 the end of the longest home winning streak in college basketball history.

The 99-game winning streak was held by Bonaventure on its official home court, the Olean Armory, that barn-like drill shed for National Guardsmen except on those winter nights when Bona played basketball. The Armory was unsuitable for basketball but it was all Bona had. A Sports Illustrated reporter not identified with a by-line described it this way:

"… the crowd that sits exactly two inches from the playing area on one side of the court, and (the visitors) ignored the balcony which projects to the edge of the other side of the playing area. The visitors seemed to revel in the way the dim light reflected off the bilious-green walls. They behaved as if this architectural monstrosity in western New York state was their own home instead of St. Bonaventure's."

The visitors that March night were Gallagher's Niagara Purple Eagles. They faced a formidable task. Bonaventure was ranked second in the national polls, a spot they'd held all season long, with only a Christmas-time loss to Number One Ohio State marring their perfect record. The Buckeyes, led by Jerry Lucas, Larry Siegfried and John Havlicek, had just edged Tom Stith and company in Madison Square Garden.

It was a sure thing that top opponents would seldom come to play Bona in the Armory. As SI reported: "The coaches of top teams refused to risk their records in what they called Bonaventure's snake pit. The school issued orders that its students must be quiet during all foul shots, an edict remarkably well obeyed. But the armory remained no place to visit and a great place to live. Donovan himself estimated the home-court advantage at from seven to 10 points."

It wasn't true that the school had issued an order to be quiet during opponent free throws. It was just a student psychological ploy, and it was eerie.

St. Bonaventure was never in the game that night, trailing by double figures most of the way, as Niagara's Al Butler hit four baskets in the last three minutes to seal the win. The final was 88-78. "Taps Gallagher, kissed his players, patted his balding head and was carried off the floor proclaiming he hadn't won a bigger game in 27 years of coaching," reported SI.

The author attended that game and can bear witness to everything written by the reporter from Sports Illustrated. In a way, it was a capstone of the decade previous, with on-court success never to be matched by all three schools at the same time. Each had its moments in decades leading to the millennium, but there has never been a time since that St. Bonaventure, Canisius and Niagara were national powers simultaneously.

Therein lies the story. What happened when obsession with a return to national prominence nearly destroyed a university, corroded its reputation and caused its basketball program to be a national joke.

Chapter Three

The president's job at St. Bonaventure was open, and the university's board of trustees would make the ultimate choice. A search committee worked for months culling through applications and suggestions from a consulting firm. The committee had winnowed the applicants to three. Interestingly, none was a Franciscan. For the first time in its history, the university would have a civilian as its president. Its final choice was Dr. Robert J. Wickenheiser.

The skinny on campus had favored another candidate. At least one member of the search committee had been cautioned about Bob Wickenheiser by an outsider who had watched the former monk ruffle faculty and administration feathers at Mount St. Mary's, let alone stick his presidential nose into the men's basketball program when he tried to get Jack Phelan to resign.

There are some Bona faculty members who to this day won't forgive Wickenheiser for his part in the basketball fiasco. But when he arrived on the campus in January, the university was in financial exigency, a polite term for what would be called functional bankruptcy in the business world. The previous president –a Franciscan priest– had been asked to resign by the trustees. Ironically he was the last Franciscan priest to hold the job on a regular basis. In the 10-month interim, the university hired a nun–Sister Alice Gallin–to serve as the acting president until Wickenheiser was chosen.

Bob Wickenheiser was an ultimate muscle man, with the fate of St. Bonaventure in his hip pocket. His muscling tactics later proved his downfall.

The biggest problem Wickenheiser faced when he took over was the faculty's understandable resistance to being fired. Because of the exigency situation, the university could lay off tenured faculty if it felt it necessary to do so. Tenure is what every academic shoots for in his or her career. Once a college professor is granted tenure, that professor has a lifetime job. It's almost impossible to be fired, short of criminal conduct.

Shortly after taking over the president's office in Hopkins Hall. Wickenheiser met with 70 faculty members, one by one, testing the waters with each about taking early retirement or voluntarily resigning. He sweet-talked or strong-armed 21 of the faculty to take one of those two routes. Three joined the Bonaventure administration, and seven became part-time instructors. At Bonaventure teaching part-time is so badly paid that most "adjunct professors" as they are called, joke that they are working for free, "sort of taking the Franciscan vow of poverty."

By May of 1994, Wickenheiser had met with his top administrators and deans to plan the next step. On May 20, a university publication called "Inside Bona" reported the president's position was that "women will not be let go, whether tenured or not, before tenured males because of the glaring lack of women on our faculty." The publication also reported: "in order to maintain a substantial friar presence, whenever possible a friar will be kept."

The Franciscans are known as friars, and they still were an integral part of the school's identity even though they didn't run it any more. To this day, Franciscans live in a handsome "friary" on campus, though few teach at the university any longer. Declining vocations and more interest among the Franciscans in working social justice issues and with the poor have reduced the number on campus to about a dozen. In 1994 there were at least twice as many at Bona, and most of them taught.

Those civilian faculty being fired were promised a year's salary plus "all benefits" that the university customarily provides. Wickenheiser next moved to cut the payroll even more. The administration announced a one-year 6.5-per cent reduction of all staff and faculty salaries, and reducing the university's 10 per cent contribution to retirement plans to 5 percent of an employee's annual pay.

The layoffs would cost Bonaventure about $2.2 million in settlements, money that the trustees indicated they would raise among themselves. Wickenheiser had trimmed the faculty, but when the freshman class arrived in the fall of 1994, it totaled 464 students, up from 375 a year before. For freshmen it meant large class sizes, something that was not the usual situation at St. Bonaventure.

Meanwhile, 11 of the male faculty who'd been terminated reacted to the decision to retain all of the women professors by filing complaints with the Equal Employment Opportunity Commission. Their complaints charged reverse discrimination in favor of women. Though Bonaventure's undergraduate enrollment was about 50 per cent women then (and remains that way today) there were only 24 women professors of the 160 faculty total before the layoffs and buyouts. Five women voluntarily retired when the university started its faculty reduction process, leaving just 19.

An American Association of University Professors, (AAUP) report summarized his first moves and added a critical comment about basketball at Bonas: "Other documents from her time (Sister Alice's) as interim president showed a strong concern for reforms in faculty governance and an awareness of a widespread sentiment among the faculty that 'the trustees have a greater commitment to basketball than to a baccalaureate degree.'"

"With the arrival of President Wickenheiser in February 1994, the pace of events accelerated. He promptly set about interviewing faculty members, some seventy in all, with a view to encouraging voluntary resignations and retirements. This effort yielded twenty- one separations from full-time status, of which three were transfers to administrative positions and seven to part-time positions. But it was not considered to be enough. In May the president, after consulting chiefly with the senior vice-presidents and deans, decided that the involuntary release of about twenty-two faculty members, of whom eighteen were tenured, was unavoidable."

Wickenheiser cut down the faculty with a pole ax, eliminating male tenured professors, but not dispatching any women faculty or Franciscans who still were teaching at Bonaventure. He was able to do this because the university was in that state of financial exigency—in effect was losing millions of dollars a year between income and expenses. If it were a private business it would have declared bankruptcy. Under this scenario, Wickenheiser was able to persuade the 20-plus faculty members to retire or switch jobs, and pulled the trigger on another 22 faculty.

The AAUP later criticized Wickenheiser, saying : "The St. Bonaventure University administration, in acting to terminate the appointments of eighteen tenured professors, proceeded in disregard" of AAUP guidelines, and that critical report still hangs over the university to this day. Nonetheless, his actions may have saved the university.

Chapter Four

In the fall of 1995, the author was employed on the new arena project in Buffalo.

Part of the plan for the Crossroads Arena, as it was known until corporate sponsorship was sold to the Marine Midland Bank (now it's known as the First Niagara Center after a takeover.) The arena was a joint project spurred by the Knox brothers, who owned the NHL Buffalo Sabres, and the City of Buffalo, Erie County and the State of New York.

Since the only major tenant of the arena was the Sabres hockey team, developer Larry Quinn and the author planned to bring about a return of major college basketball to downtown Buffalo. We called the concept the "Big Four" a name adapted from Philadelphia's five Division One college teams who played each other annually.

In this case the Big Four would be Canisius, Niagara the University at Buffalo (which was just moving into college basketball's competitive ranks with entry into the MAC along with schools such as Bowling Green and Toledo,) and finally, St. Bonaventure.

The author had grown up watching Bona, Canisius and Niagara in the phenomenally successful Saturday night doubleheader program in old Memorial Auditorium, and believed it could happen again in the new Crossroads facility. The key school was Bonaventure, for the teams from Allegany had reached national prominence more consistently than the others.

In the mid-90s Canisius was still playing some games in the Aud, and more in a band-box gym on campus. The other schools were also on campus for all or mosthome games.

The University at Buffalo, a state school that is by far the largest of the quartet, had a 9000-capacity bleacher arena on campus, and didn't really need seating. But UB officials felt that the exposure of playing in the Crossroads situation would be good for recruiting. Niagara was playing in the Taps Gallagher Center on its Lewiston campus, a 2300-seat bleacher building.

Bonaventure's home games were being played in the Reilly Center on campus. It held seats for 4400, most of them theater-back and comfortable. Bona rarely played in Buffalo, and always against Canisius in Memorial Aud.

The Canisius coach that year was John Beilein, now the head coach at the University of Michigan. In meetings with Quinn and the author, Beilein was enthusiastic about the plans for a Big Four basketball program in the new arena. The plans were fluid, but basically called for each of the four to play the other three during the season, plus play one "marquee" game against a nationally known opponent. In the beginning, there wouldn't be doubleheaders, but that possibility still was there in the future.

Niagara's coach, Jack Armstrong, also supported the Big Four proposal, as did Tim Cohane from UB. There were no major down sides, insisted the author in a series of meetings with each of the schools' athletic directors. Handshakes followed, and informal letters of agreement exchanged with Canisius, Niagara and UB. But Bonaventure was a different story.

Bona's athletic director appointed earlier in the year was Dave Diles, son of a very popular Michigan radio and tv sports announcer. Diles was hesitant in our first meeting and ensuing phone calls. He seemed afraid to take any kind of position about the proposal for a Big Four. Diles had no background in the long and successful Bonaventure culture of basketball (including those doubleheader years in Buffalo) and pointed out that the Bonnies had the Reilly Center, where they played Atlantic 10 Conference foes and a few others.

"It would only be four appearances in Buffalo in the first two or three years," he was told by the author. "You wouldn't have to play any conference home games away from your campus building." Diles wouldn't be pinned down with any answer. Finally, he said we'd have to talk to the president.

"You mean Bob Wickenheiser makes decisions on your basketball program?" he was asked. "You better talk to Dr. Wickenheiser," he repeated.

The author talked with Quinn about Diles refusal to even negotiate about Bona in Buffalo, and Quinn tried to pry him loose with a phone call.

He got the same response, so the author decided he would talk to Wicken-heiser himself.

(Author's disclosure: I had already met Bob as a member of the university's Advisory Council to the President on Mass Communication, and as a Bonaventure alumnus figured I would have the best chance to get him interested in Buffalo. I phoned his office and only reached his administrative assistant, Joan Zink, who served in that role for many Bona presidents before Wickenheiser came on board. I explained my position to Ms. Zink, and told her Dave Diles had steered me to her boss. When I couldn't even get a phone call through to him, I knew we were in trouble.)

A few days later Ms. Zink phoned me to inform us that no face-to-face meeting was possible due the "president's busy schedule" but that he would talk to the author by phone the next day.

That phone call marked the end of the Big Four basketball program in the Crossroads Arena.

"Why would I bring Bonaventure to play in Buffalo," Wickenheiser said in opening up his end of the conversation. "I have a perfectly good arena on campus, a schedule that brings some of the best teams in the country here, and a student body that supports the team."

Explaining that four games in Buffalo—including an annual marquee opponent from the SEC, ACC or Big East—would only increase Bona visibility in the college basketball world, didn't impress the president one bit. "I don't want our students coming all the way to Buffalo, getting drunk and getting into auto accidents or worse," he said.

Wickenheiser had a good point. Bona students were notorious for their drinking. Once in the 90s the school was named seventh best in party schools across the country by a group that rates that sort of thing. Drunken college boys and girls strewn along the roadside on the 70-mile stretch between the Bona campus and downtown Buffalo would be a public relations nightmare.

Yet Bona students had been coming to Buffalo for more than a decade after World War Two, and there were no disasters, though there was steady beer-drinking every doubleheader weekend.

We were never sure whether Wickenheiser had discussed the idea in any length with Coach Jim Baron or with Diles. One has to assume he did, but what happened to the Bona basketball program in the pages to follow indicate it was Wickenheiser's decision. He was involved in basketball up to his elbows then, deciding where Bona would play and in effect, who they would play, by excluding the team from a round-robin with the other three Western New York colleges.

Journalists liked the name "Big Four" so much that to this day, many refer to games involving the four schools as just that, a "Big Four" contest. Quinn tried to get Bona to come in with another series of phone calls to Diles and Wickenheiser, offering some compromises that would have been unfair to the other three schools. He had no luck, but managed to get the people at Canisius, Niagara and UB angry.

Niagara improved the Gallagher Center, and still plays all home games there. Canisius remodeled its tiny gym facility and plays every home game there but one annual appearance on the HSBC "Big Four" basketball floor. UB has improved its on-campus arena, and plays all its home games there.

The preceding isn't a criticism of Wickenheiser's decision to stay away from the Big Four concept. It is revealing though, that he was directly and totally in charge of the basketball fortunes at Bonaventure in 1995, a year after he became president.

Bob Wickenheiser was an ultimate fan, with the fate of Bona's program in his hip pocket. And it later proved his downfall.

Chapter Five

Jan van Breda Kolff was one of those college basketball coaches who had succeeded at every level. He's the son of an NBA star of the past, Butch van Breda Kolff, who played with the New York Knicks for four seasons, and later coached four NBA teams including two Los Angeles Laker squads that reached the NBA finals.

Jan was an outstanding forward at Vanderbilt University, named the player of the year in his senior year as he led the Commodores to the SEC title. He later played for teams in the defunct American Basketball League and the NBA.

At 6 foot 7 inches tall, Jan was an angular forward, with a fair shot and a high level of intensity in his play. He was a perfect personality candidate to become a college coach, since college basketball coaches tend to be driven personalities, obsessive and not easy to get along with.

That's because they are in a high-stakes business, particularly at the Division One level. There are 347 head coaching jobs in Division One (D-1) and the top 20 or so make salaries hovering around the million-dollar mark. Even a school as small as St. Bonaventure pays its coach nearly 2 ½ times what the president of the university makes in base salary.

It's exceptionally rare that any coach stays with a D-1 program for his entire career. It's rare that they stay more than a few years. If they are successful, they find a job with another school that will pay them more. If they aren't successful in the eyes of fans, boosters and their university bosses, they get fired. Since no one hopes to be fired from a job in six figures, coaches are obsessively paranoiac, convinced that they are the center of the campus universe.

That doesn't mean they can't be charming and friendly. In fact, some of the most successful coaches are that way because of their ability to schmooze with parents of kids they're trying to recruit, and with boosters who'll give large donations to the "program."

That's what nearly every coach calls his basketball situation: "the program." Doing so separates it from the rest of the college or university where he's employed. It's as if basketball at St. Bonaventure or Ohio State was a different function than college education, instead of part of that education.

The fact is that college basketball and college football at the D-1 level are entirely different from the business of education. They're as close to professional sports as one could determine what professional means. Even at a school like Bonaventure, with an enrollment of 2000 undergraduates, the basketball "program" is distinctly separate from university life, except on those home game nights when hundreds of students cram special bleacher seating.

The rest of the time basketball exists in a world of its own. The players live together, eat together, travel together, and in many cases go to class together because a majority are enrolled in what they are told is the least difficult major on campus. And why is this area of study considered the easiest for basketball players? It's mainly because there are more elective hours than other majors, and athletes love electives. They mean softer courses and teacher hunting (a practice where a student searches for a course based on a perception that the professor is an easy grader.)

So "the program" existed at St. Bonaventure when van Breda Kolff was hired in 2001 to succeed Jim Baron, a Bona alumnus and basketball player at the school who was not Wickenheiser's favorite. Baron wanted more money and the president wasn't willing to pay him anything close to what he asked, so he moved on—as coaches do—taking over a struggling program at the University of Rhode Island. Baron's move was unusual in that he moved to another "program" in the same conference, the Atlantic Ten and, as is the standard practice, both Baron and URI were required to request permission from SBU to speak with each other about the position. URI did not contact SBU for permission until the day of the press conference of Baron's hiring at URI. As if we should be surprised.

Van Breda Kolff moved to Bonaventure from Pepperdine University in California, where he had been the winner of three quarters of his games as a coach in two seasons. He had also been successful at his alma mater, Vanderbilt, and at his first head coaching job at Cornell University. Pepperdine was a stop along the way in the progression coaches usually make.

Then why St. Bonaventure next? He had applied for the job and was one of the three finalists that a search committee had locked in on. It seemed at best a lateral move, a step up in conference, but not necessarily a step up in the "program." Bonaventure had one of the smaller basketball budgets in the A-10, and it was not likely to increase substantially under a new coach. One of Baron's complaints other than his own salary was about the total resources allotted to the program.

Van Breda Kolff scored the biggest contract ever given a Bonaventure coach, hiring on with a package of salary and benefits totaling $325,000 a year. Baron's package was not much more than half that. Wickenheiser decided that van Breda Kolff was the guy for the job for reasons of his own. One of them may have been the kind of assistant coaches van Breda Kolff was going to hire. Presto, one of van Breda Kolff's hires as an assistant was Kort Wickenheiser, the president's son.

Though he never openly discussed it, the story on campus about why van Breda Kolff took the Bona job is that he wanted to be closer to his family, who all lived on the east coast.

The first thing the new coach had to do—like anyone who gets a job in a different place—was to find a place to live. Depending on your taste and budget, finding the right place near St. Bonaventure's handsome campus can be difficult. The town of Allegany is actual location of St. Bonaventure, and the Village of Allegany abuts the campus. Both the town and the village have limited housing stock of the kind a six-figure coach might like, at least this coach.

The small city of Olean is to the east of the campus. With about 18,000 residents and a declining economy, Olean has some handsome old homes, but many more on the same streets that are sagging in disrepair. There is one subdivision of more expensive homes. Apparently none of these appealed to the new coach. He extended his search to the northwest, zeroing in one a small ski town named Ellicottville, that bills itself as "the Aspen of the East."

The search with a real estate agent took van Breda Kolff through hillside chalets that were second residences for wealthy Canadians and midwest-erners as well as a large group from the Buffalo area, just 50 miles north. Some of the homes were priced near the $1-million dollar mark, very high in western New York, which has some of the lowest real estate prices in the country.

Van Breda Kolff didn't see anything he liked until riding with the agent he passed one house. He is said to have told the agent to pull over. He liked the large chalet-style house but was told it wasn't for sale. Van Breda Kolff went to the door instead, and in a few minutes made an offer to buy from a surprised home owner, who also first insisted the house wasn't for sale.

But van Breda Kolff got his way with her by upping the price to a number she and her husband couldn't refuse. He got the house. The previous owners hurriedly moved, bought another place in the ski village, and banked a big profit.

The coach was used to getting his way. A lawn service company that he hired to take care of his property became so angry with the way he treated its employees that it spread the word to competitors. It wasn't long before no local lawn service outfits would service the new Bonaventure coach.

The second piece of the machinery that brought Bona to its knees was in place; a coach who knew his job and who had been hired to win now, or at least very soon. The coach was imperious and driven, distant except with his staff and players, but certainly distant with the university community. He had his "program," and he was hired to make it nationally prominent. Soon he was joined by the president's son, Kort Wickenheiser, coming in as a coach and recruiter.

Chapter Six

Barbara Questa came to St. Bonaventure and its Athletics Department in 1992, after a one-year stint as assistant commissioner of the East Coast Conference, a year as an intern in Syracuse University's Athletics Department and a master's degree in sports psychology from Temple University. She also attended Temple as an undergraduate.

By 1998 she had been promoted to senior associate athletics director at Bonaventure, and was the department's expert in compliance with the rules and regulations of the NCAA. Between the time she came to Bona and 2001, when van Breda Kolff was hired, the men's basketball program had a clean slate as far as any major violations of the NCAA's arcane rules and regulations. In fact, it was her attention to the detail and rigor of the rules that kept her a valued member of the staff no matter who was the athletics director. As of this writing, she holds her job.

It's difficult to do it by the book when facing the NCAA rules even under the best of conditions. When a school or part of its athletics apparatus decides to try and skirt the rules, particularly in recruiting, it's up to the NCAA compliance officer to say no. Ms. Questa was the Bonaventure official who usually said no. That's what the various athletics directors expected from her. The NCAA regulations are her mantra.

In 1999, Bonaventure had advertised for a new AD when Dave Diles resigned to take a similar job at his alma mater, Eastern Michigan University. Among the applications was one from an athletic administrator at the University of Maryland named Gothard Lane.

Lane had been a football player at Randolph-Macon College where he received a bachelor's degree in English. He joined the football coaching staff at Maryland shortly thereafter, then moved on to front office duties, eventually becoming the Associate Athletic Director for Varsity Sports. He stayed with the Terrapins for 25 years.

Lane saw an ad for the Bona job and, after interviewing with members of a search committee, was hired by Wickenheiser in the early fall 1999.

"He had a reputation for being very excited about basketball, very impassioned about it. I knew that because he'd been the president of Mount St. Mary's College University in Emmitsburg, Maryland. And so I knew he was very supportive of basketball and he seemed like a nice guy when I met him," Lane recalled.

He took over a department that was always funded less than its status in 16 Division One sports competition deserved. That situation continues to this day, as Bonaventure's financial troubles continue into this decade.

Lane is one of a dying breed, those who wear blue blazers, tan slacks, button-down shirts and exhibit what some would describe as prep school manners. In his case, Lane's gracious exterior extended to his work, and he was well liked by the staff and interns who worked under him at Bonaventure. He could be firm and authoritative, but even then remained polite and gracious. He would need every social and work skill, it turned out, to survive what was to come on the campus.

Right away he had to deal with the intense Baron, the men's basketball coach. In that first season, Baron's team received a bid to the NCAA tournament, and followed with a bid to the NIT in 2000-2001. Baron was looking for a new contract, seeking a substantial raise, even though his teams had only begun winning regularly in those last two years. Wickenheiser didn't particularly like Baron and made no special effort to keep him. Just a few weeks after Baron left for Rhode Island, van Breda Kolff was hired by Lane with the president's approval in April of 2001.

" I think he had been a very capable coach. He'd been successful at every school he'd coached at. So if that's what you're looking for, you're looking for how he was successful, not just at one place that could be luck of the draw but he coached at Cornell, Vanderbilt and Pepperdine and won at all three places so therefore we thought he was a good choice. And he was extremely bright. A very good bench coach, court coach, everybody said. But a lot of basketball coaches are all are a little strange. They're all very hyper, very focused on what they're doing. They can be tough to deal with," said Lane.

In the beginning Lane didn't notice much of a change working with van Breda Kolff compared to Baron. " He was like Jimmy Baron in a lot of ways. With all high profile coaches in basketball, you can't do enough for them.

Nothing's ever quite right. There's always a new demand, you know, that type of thing," he said.

There is always a pressure today on the coach of the men's basketball team at Bonaventure. But it wasn't that way when the school's first run of national prominence came under Eddie Donovan. The late Bona coach was nicknamed "Wacky" by the media and fans of the program because he was very excitable on the bench during games, to put it mildly.

Eddie would stalk the referees (there were two then) up and down the side-line when he had a complaint about a call. He was a feisty Irishman from Eliza-beth, New Jersey who had graduated from Bona in 1950 and stayed around the area, coaching Olean High School's boys team. In 1953 he was tapped for the head coaching job at Bona, the only coaching job at Bona. He had a part-time assistant, a 1953 graduate, Bob Sassone, who'd been one of the best play-ers along with Mal Duffy in Bonaventure's teams shortly after the war.

Donovan was a gregarious sort, with a passion for the game and that excitable sideline persona. He was also a good recruiter, though recruit-ing in the late 50s was unlike the high-pressure business it is today. His first "star" was a squint-eyed guard named Brendan McCann, whose eyesight was so poor he had to wear glasses to read off the board when he sat in class. McCann was a fine ball handler who once confessed that he never saw the rim and net clearly when he let go a set shot. "Set shots" for those who don't remember, were taken with two hands pushing the ball off the chest, and usually were set up by a pick. McCann became a first-round draft choice of the New York Knicks in 1957, but his shot or his vision didn't match up to NBA standards.

By the late 1950's Donovan's teams were consistent and good; good enough to make the NIT every year through 1960, and the NCAA tourna-ment in 1961. Donovan was lucky enough to get Tom and Sam Stith from St. Francis Prep in Brooklyn, followed by Freddie Crawford from the same high school. He was good enough to mold each team into a top 20 competi-tor, even before the arrival of the Brooklyn contingent. Eddie took the team on the road alone, except for the sports publicist, Jack Ritzenthaler, who also doubled as the road manager, arranging travel, meals, etc.

In 1959, St. Bonaventure was away late in the season at Providence Col-lege for an important game involving national ranking for both schools. PC was one of Bonaventure's natural rivalries. The Dominican college and the Franciscan university were small and very Catholic, with most courses taught by men in the two religious orders. Providence was led by one of smoothest guards in the country, Lenny Wilkins, who starred in the NBA and then coached for decades in the same league.

The game was scheduled in PC's on-campus gymnasium, and was sold out. That didn't stop the author and three of his friends from wanting to be there. That's where the difference between college basketball then, and basketball "programs" today can easily be illustrated. One the day of the game, four of us piled into my car with enough money for gas to make it to Providence. We drove the 400-plus miles and arrived late in the afternoon at the campus, and head for the gym's box office.

"No tickets left, boys. Sorry," said the man behind the window. With little money, and no tickets, it appeared out 400-mile journey to follow our school's team was going to be fruitless. Then we spotted Ritzenthaler walking into the building. We rushed up to him and identified ourselves and asked if he could help. "I'll talk to Eddie and we'll see what we can do," he said. "Meet me back here at 6:30."

We had no place to go and not enough money to buy dinner, so we walked around the campus and returned to meet him and find out what was to come next. Jack took us into the gym and the coach was there. "Guys, I can't find any tickets for you," said Donovan. "Geez, though, it's great that you came all this way to see the game. So here's what I am going to do."

That evening, we watched the game from the far end of the Bonaventure bench. Donovan wasn't traveling a big squad anyway. There were only eight scholarship players on the team. We were self-conscious at first, though we personally knew every player and were friends with half of them. We just felt that we stuck out like sore thumbs at the end of the bench.

The story had a happy ending of a sort. Providence beat Bona soundly, and when it was over Coach Donovan invited the four of us to come along with the team and join them for a post-game meal in the back of a local tavern. It didn't cost us a dime, and was a good thing, as we didn't have many dimes at that point. Friendly PC students bought us beers afterward, and we slept on the hard floors of student dormitories that night. Before we left the tavern, Ritzenthaler asked us if we were sure we had enough money to make it back to campus.

It's not likely any coach in today's basketball "programs" would even pay attention if he ran into students today doing what we did. And it's even less likely anybody would sit on the bench.

In Donovan's days at St. Bonaventure there was a culture of personal student support for his teams. Players were part of the general student population. They were spread among many majors and nearly everyone attended classes with basketball players. The student body was small, about 800 men and 50 women, and the entire male student body ate meals at the same time in the university dining hall, (women weren't allowed in the dining hall and there were no women's dorms.) Basketball players lived in the same dorms as the rest of the students (they still do) and there was such a thing as "school spirit."

Bonaventure's most hated rival was Canisius, followed by Niagara. There had been college boy pranks involving each of the schools the week before rivalry games in years past. Students from one school would raid the opponent's campus during the night, whitewashing statues, putting up insulting signs, stealing some icon, and generally doing silly college boy things with little or no damage. In 1951, the presidents of the three colleges pleaded for the raiding to stop after three Niagara students died when their plane crashed on its way to drop leaflets onto the Bonaventure campus before a game.

Bonaventure teams were known as the "Brown Indians" in those days, the brown coming from the color of Franciscan garb, known as the "habit" by the friars. The Indian part came from the location of the university on land adjacent to the reservation land of the Seneca tribe.

The nickname came into being in 1927, but was never officially adopted until 1961, apparently in an attempt to justify the university's use of what some felt was an insult to Native Americans. A student in full buckskin and full western head dress was on the arena for every home basketball game. Being named the "Brown Indian" was an honor sought by many students. In 1967, Bonaventure added a "Brown Squaw," a woman student who wore an ersatz Indian costume and was also at every home game.

During Father Neil's tenure as president, the university reached out to the Senecas nearby by inviting them to buy into the Brown Indian nickname. A Seneca artist actually painted a center court representation of member of the tribe on the Reilly Center floor. In the mid-90s the NCAA made its first sweeping moves to eliminate college team nicknames representing Native Americans, ruling them insulting and demeaning. In 1996, the Wickenheiser administration ordered the nickname to disappear from Bona sports teams.

In the place came the "Bonnies," a nickname that has no meaning. Its derivation comes from the use of "Bonas" for "Bonaventure," a shortened word that eventually corrupted from the short "a" to the plural of a long "e." In 2010, women's basketball coach Jim Crowley told SBU-TV, the campus tv news program, that he was tired and amused by being taunted during road games when other student sections would shout in unison: "What's a Bonnie? What's a Bonnie?"

In a lame effort to succeed the Brown Indian, the school created the "Bona Fanatic," a costumed creature with none of the appeal of the Phillies Fanatic. It was often booed by the home fans and assaulted by thrown objects from the student section in the Reilly Center. The "Fanatic" had to go, so in 1999 came the "Wolfpack," but not as a team nickname. Instead, the "Bonnies" continues and the student section is sometimes called the Wolfpack, other times the "Reilly Rowdies." A new court mascot was invented, the "Bona Wolf," with a student prowling the sidelines in a wolfish costume at home games. The university introduced the wolf character as a representation of St. Francis of Assisi, the founder of the Franciscans, who was said to hang out with wolves on his way to sainthood.

Diles was still the athletics director when the Wolf made its debut. He described the character as "aggressive, yet friendly; leaner and more athletic than previous representations." Apparently that meant all the Brown Indians and Squaws who preceded the animal.

The subject is best left to further exploration by sociologists.

Chapter Seven

Four of the key figures were all in place by the spring of 2002: Wickenheiser, Lane, Questa, and van Breda Kolff. Another who looms important in the story had also been hired by van Breda Kolff as an assistant coach. Kort Wickenheiser, one of the president's five children, had two years' experience as an assistant at Wagoner College and four years at DeMatha Catholic High School in Washington, DC, one of the renowned high school basketball powers in the country.

Kort had graduated from Muhlenberg College either summa or magna cum laude with a B.S. in chemistry and philosophy, a pre-med program. In one source—the 2001-2002 media guide from St. Bonaventure men's basketball– he's listed as a "summa," while his current on-line business profile lists him as "magna." Small thing, but there is a difference. He was captain of the Muhlenberg Centennial Conference championship team.

It was a common belief on the Bonaventure campus that Kort Wickenheiser's employment as a basketball assistant was part of van Breda Kolff's deal with the school. Nearly every single figure in the chapters that follow either told the author or testified to that belief before an internal Bonaventure investigating committee or the NCAA. But he had some real props. He was a chemistry and biology teacher at DeMatha and served two years as the freshman coach under the legendary Morgan Wootten. His freshman record was 50-2 and he also was a varsity assistant.

Nonetheless, the hiring of Kort Wickenheiser by van Breda Kolff was greeted with laughter by many faculty who scoffed at the notion that he just "happened" to get the job while his father was the university president.

Make no mistake about Bob Wickenheiser and college basketball. He was a passionate fan, and a loud one. From his center court seats at the Reilly Center, Bob Wickenheiser often shouted vitriol-laced invective at any referee who dared to make a call against Bona, or when a call wasn't made that he felt should have been. Wickenheiser was on his feet some nights more than he sat down, yelling as loudly as anyone in the building.

Bob Wickenheiser told the author in the spring of 2008 that he hadn't much liked van Breda Kolff's predecessor, Jim Baron, and was happy to see him move on. He didn't say if he'd tried to keep him. Baron was a popular Bona coach because he was an alumnus, and co-captain of the Bonnies 1977 NIT champions. Whether Baron was offered a new contract by Wickenheiser, or not, he acted quickly when the season was over in March of 2001, signing on the University of Rhode Island.

Less than a month later, van Breda Kolff was hired at Bona after quick action by a search committee. Lane said he had applied for the job, and had not been head hunted.

Bob Wickenheiser's basketball fervor was reflected in the basketball media guide that came out in the fall of that year. In addition to a glowing three-page biography of the new head coach, there's a page and picture allotted to the president who was entering his ninth year at the top at Bonaventure and credited with forging "an exciting vision… as it (the university) enters the new millennium, while strengthening its core mission and values."

A survey of media guides from that year at other D-1 schools didn't turn up any others that had a page on the college president. Then Bona had a basketball junkie for a president.

Van Breda Kolff's first year as coach was relatively successful. The Bonnies finished 8-8 in the Atlantic 10, and 17-13 over all. Led by guard J.R. Bremer, the team was a win shy of the 18-12 record that Baron had posted in his last year as coach.. After winning against Duquesne in the first round of the conference tournament, St. Bonaventure lost to the University of Richmond in the second round and was sent packing.

The 2001-02 season also included a huge upset of the nationally ranked University of Connecticut Huskies 88-70 on UConn's home court, that sent shockwaves around college basketball country. It was after this win that Wickenheiser's interest and expectations for the program increased.

College basketball coaches lead double lives by necessity. Barely had van Breda Kolff ending his pacing in front of the Bona bench in the tournament when he and his staff were concentrating on obtaining the next additions to the "program," players recruited to come to the Allegany campus in the fall. They could be coming in as freshmen, or in another common recruiting practice, from two years at a junior college.

Many of the best players coming out of high school each spring are also the worst students. Some of them go off to prep schools to get high enough SAT scores so they can "qualify" for a scholarship according to NCAA regulations. The qualification standard then, as now, is remarkably low, but dozens of blue-chip basketball prospects leave high school with SAT's so low they need prep school or the other alternative, the junior college route.

One of those junior college prospects was a 6-8 forward from Coastal Georgia Community College, Jamil Terrell, the player whose presence later on would complete the central cast of the St. Bonaventure scandal. "It wasn't a recruiting scandal," said Lane in an interview with the author. "It was an academic scandal."

President Wickenheiser, the university's chief academic officer, decided to admit Terrell to the university and also was the person who contacted Dr. Skip Saal, SBU Vice President for Academic Affairs, to have Jamil Terrell's grade changed.

Terrell had drawn the interest of many college coaches in the east. He was strong, ran the floor well, and had at least adequate shooting and rebounding skills for a player his size. But most of the other schools were hanging back from Terrell because of his course of study at the Georgia school.

"He had to have 35 per cent of his course work transferred here (Bonaventure) to be immediately eligible," Kort Wickenheiser later told the NCAA. "Barbara Questa thought it looked hard because there were basic math concepts, appreciation of arts, plus a number of welding classes on his transcript, which was untypical. It raised the red flag right away and Barb was skeptical."

Terrell was heavily involved in the welding courses at Coastal, and lightly involved in the more traditional side of academic endeavor, the kind that is usually required to complete a bachelor's degree. That's what scared away many recruiters. They felt he either wouldn't be eligible to play after transfer, or he wouldn't stay eligible. Not that there aren't dozens of cases in every conference each year of basketball players recruited and admitted despite very questionable academic records. Division One coaches, under the gun to win so they can keep collecting six-and-seven-figure salaries, usually aren't concerned with a student's academic progress.

As long as the player stays eligible to play, the coach's concerns begin and end with his "program." Consequently every athletics department has at least one staff person in charge of making sure players stay eligible, through course and major selection and through tutoring. They're the people who find the easiest possible majors for athletes who struggle in school. Sometimes those majors also include professors who are jock sniffers themselves, and gladly hand out grades to athletes that they really didn't earn. Every school has faculty members like that, though they all deny it.

And if pressure comes down from the top, those same professors feel the heat and act upon it.

In 2002 just that kind of pressure came down from Bob Wickenheiser who intervened in the case of J.R. Bremer's quest for a degree, or more accurately in his mother's hope that her basketball-playing son would get that bachelor's degree.

Bremer was enrolled as a marketing major in the Bonaventure School of Business, an accredited and respected part of the university structure. By the end of his final semester, Bremer was already property of the NBA Boston Celtics and focused on making that team in training camps. There were workouts and pre-training camp sessions for rookies like Bremer, so he was away from campus often in the final few weeks of the spring semester. The result was a pair of "incompletes," grades that stand for what they appear to stand for, meaning he hadn't finished the requirements of two courses. Without those courses, Bremer couldn't graduate.

Bob Wickenheiser had promised Bremer's mother when he was recruited that J.R would earn his Bonaventure degree and had met with her on graduation weekend when Bremer joined his classmates in academic gown and mortarboard at the ceremonies in the Reilly Center. Bremer was allowed to "walk" at graduation because it was customary to allow that for seniors who were just a course or two short of a degree. The "graduate" received an empty diploma case and no one among the crowd was the wiser except the student and his family.

Bremer's academic advisor in the School of Business was Dr. Michael Russell, the head of the marketing degree program. Mike is a no-nonsense guy, who happens to be married to Barbara Russell, at that time the registrar of the university, the gatekeeper job in determining a student's academic profile. Mrs. Russell comes into the story more directly in a later chapter.

Bob Wickenheiser called Mike Russell. "Bob basically asked what was going on with regard to that incomplete," Russell told the NCAA. "He opened the conversation with to the effect of, what do you know about Todd Palmer." The president was enquiring about the professor who had entered one of Bremer's incomplete grades. Palmer was in his first year on the faculty and had come from the deep south, where Bonaventure basketball had no profile.

Bremer had been in a Palmer course on business practices and was with a group of students who were to do their final project together. He hadn't pitched in with the group and Dr. Palmer called Bremer in for a come-to-Jesus meeting about it. At the meeting Palmer gave Bremer an alternate assignment to complete so he could get a grade in the course. He told the NCAA that Bremer later turned something in but "I looked at it and I said: well, jeez, this isn't what I want."

Bremer complained that he had done a paper, but Palmer reminded him that the paper would have to be satisfactory to get through the course.

Palmer was married a few weeks later, and when he returned to the campus from his honeymoon he picked up a phone message from Mike Russell that he said was "Todd, you better come down here. I just got a call from the university president and he said: 'There's a situation going on.' I thought, holy heck, what kind of a situation."

He met with Dr. Russell and Mike Fisher, the business school dean, in Russell's office." Nobody was telling me to do anything at this point," Palmer testified. "...the main message I got from, that Wickenheiser delivered to Mike Russell is, 'Don't worry, we'll take care of this'."

'I had basically worked my ass for the last year for the university and I'm thinking, you know, is this gonna jeopardize my job? I mean, I've just started this thing on values and ethics in the Business School...talk about being in a very strange position."

Palmer was not a tenured professor at that time. In fact he was working on an annual contract that had to be offered and approved by the university president. He testified that Russell, Fisher and Skip Saal all told him they had his back whatever he decided to do about Bremer's grade. Palmer told investigators that Bremer could be given a "D" grade based on the sum total of his work in the semester. "I was definitely on the losing hand. So he made a 'D.' I'll give him a 'D'"

"I knew that if I gave him an F, he would not have graduated," Palmer said.

"I was totally shell shocked at what Wickenheiser had done." Records show that Palmer turned in the "D" grade on Sept. 4. But Bremer's official transcript shows that he was granted his degree four days earlier, on Aug. 31. There is no explanation for this discrepancy.

Palmer testified: "The president, in my opinion, violated the chain of command. What was communicated to me was vague, but I would take it as sort of intimidating....This is not the place a first-year non- tenure professor wants to be in.

"It was (an) almost push from God-type thing...really spooked me... I sort of view myself as sort of a victim in all this, and just like...holy cow... did I do the right thing?"

The other professor involved in Wickenheiser's pressure job to get Bremer his degree was an adjunct, Kevin Brayer. In his testimony, Brayer said he taught a course in the fall of 2001 in which Bremer earned an "I", a grade of incomplete, because he didn't do the final project. This involved shadowing a salesman, and was worth 20 to 30 per cent of the grade.

After Mike Russell told Brayer the president was anxious to get the "I " changed to a grade so Bremer could graduate, Brayer said he agreed through Russell to give Bremer until Nov. 1 to complete the work and turned in a "B" for the basketball player.

Bremer never contacted him or did the work. But once the degree was granted it couldn't be taken back.

Brayer was asked by the NCAA's Higgins how this happened. "Because I truly had felt that because of the values and the principles that we teach here, (and) because of the maturity that I had seen on J.R.'s part that he would do the responsible and right thing."

Higgins: "OK. Did you ever set up this sort of arrangement before?"
Brayer: "No."
Higgins: Would you ever consider doing it again?
Brayer: "No."
"I've never been put in this position before," Brayer concluded.

Wickenheiser had put the heat on to a non-tenured first-year professor, and an adjunct (a part-timer) to get his basketball star a degree he never earned. Wick was relatively subtle when he put people like Mike Russell and Mike Fisher on the spot with his pressure tactics. Both had told Palmer they'd back his decision, but they knew that if the president didn't get his way he played hard ball.

Chapter Eight

In the fall of 2001, Dr. Joseph Greer, a 30-year sociology professor at Bonaventure had a section of one of his courses that he'll never forget. Greer was not surprised that two of his students were varsity basketball players when he scanned his class roster, as many of the team were sociology majors, and he's had plenty of experience with this breed of varsity athletes in the past.

When you teach varsity athletes at Bonaventure, each must provide a schedule from the athletics department indicating when he'll be away traveling and playing his sport's road schedule. It can be irritating to the professor if an athlete is traveling over testing periods, and special assignments and deadlines must be made up in their consideration. But it's not so bad when the athlete is a good student, and willing to take on the imposing dual workload of being both student and varsity athlete.

That hasn't been the way with men's basketball at St. Bonaventure. Typically the cumulative grade average in any give semester by members of the team barely scrapes the 2.0 mark, a "C" average. There are usually one or two walk-ons at Bonaventure, bright-eyed ex-high school players who are scrimmage fodder and never play. Their real value to the team comes from their grades, which are normally good enough to raise the overall team average. Not only are grades important to coaches and players within a college's academic structure, low grade point averages and graduation rates can get a school in trouble with the NCAA.

Elite sports "programs" such as those at Duke don't have this problem. These "programs" have the choice of the best high school players both athletically and academically when they recruit. A faculty member at Bonaventure once asked current men's coach Mark Schmidt why Bona didn't get players with good academic records "like they have at Duke." Schmidt diplomatically replied that he would take every "A" student he could get who could play basketball.

Unfortunately, many of today's D-1 college basketball players have their eyes on a different prize than a college degree. Some in the elite "programs" stay in college just a year before declaring for the NBA draft. That's because the pro league won't let them turn pro right out of high school any more. Others are shooting for a contract to play pro ball in Europe, where six-figure contracts are routine for U.S. college players, or in other countries on other continents where the salaries are still quite attractive for a few months work.

St. Bonaventure doesn't have the pick of the litter when recruiting men's basketball players. The handsome rural campus is just that— very rural– a completely different atmosphere from which most D-1 players originate. City boys with hip-hop style, from high schools bigger than Bona's enrollment, are easily turned off when they visit the campus and find out only about 10 per cent of the student body are minorities. The nearby city— Olean— is about half that at five per cent. There is little minority culture or presence at St. Bonaventure, despite sincere effort by the current president to improve on the situation.

So in 2000, as today, minority members of the men's basketball team tended to hang together. Facing 20 hours of practice or playing time a week also produces solidarity on a team, or insularity. All the players hang out with each other by necessity, if not by choice.

Dr. Greer, in for the long haul already, was called to Bob Wickenheiser's office when the semester ended and told by the president that he was fired. A shocked Greer wanted to know why and was told that he had made racist remarks in his class, obviously directed at the two athletes. The official charges involved professional incompetence and neglect of duties, plus 11 more. Wickenheiser had booted a tenured professor out the door without warning, and without hearing his side or calling for an investigation by an impartial body, in this case the university's faculty senate.

The campus buzzed with rumors about what really happened. Because of confidentiality entitlement, the students were never publicly identified and the full details never were made public. It was ironic that Greer, who had campaigned for the Rev. Jesse Jackson in a presidential primary, and routinely assigned reading materials sympathetic to black causes, was in Wickenheiser's crosshairs. "I've been accused of being a racist," Greer told The Bona Venture, the student weekly newspaper. "I am denying all charges."

But it's safe to say that Dr. Greer was in the president's crosshairs because Wickenheiser believed he had gone after basketball players in one of his classes. The president's direct interest in basketball doesn't necessarily mean he was wrong to go after a professor he believed in violation of the university's code of ethics. The way he did it, and what happened afterward reveal that Bob Wickenheiser was more than a tough president. He was an autocrat.

The faculty senate investigation into Greer's firing went on for six months with 40 witnesses heard over 28 hours of testimony. Witnesses included several students who were in Greer's class when he was alleged to have used the "N" word. Several current faculty members who were on campus when Greer was fired told the author they believed Greer's case was a setup by members of the athletics department staff who disliked him because of his grading of basketball players.

The faculty senate report blasted Dr. Wickenheiser: It said "the president's decision was precipitous and appears to have been made with one-sided and limited information."

Wickenheiser told the media he had no plans to take the matter before the university's board of trustees, and Greer said doing so on his part would be "moot." According to the June 21 Buffalo News Greer told the paper "a letter from a university attorney after the faculty panel issued its findings offered to buy Greer out for $150,000."

Greer said he was going to sue Bonaventure, and he did file a lawsuit. The university eventually settled for an amount believed far beyond the $150,000 mark.

"There are deep flaws in the university's evaluation, assessment, and complaint processes that precluded Dr. Greer from learning of complaints against him up until the time of his dismissal," according to the faculty senate report.

That and Bob Wickenheiser's quick trigger.

Chapter Nine

It's curious that the principals in this story are all gone from the university today, yet Wickenheiser's influence still remains in a sense of edginess among many of the faculty and staff.

One incident that shows his rather Prussian way of handling matters regardless of the fallout came just a year or so into his tenure as the president. The journalism department at St. Bonaventure was headed by Dr. Russell J. Jandoli, who had founded the program after World War II and whose name graces the Jandoli School of Journalism/Mass Communication that operates today.

Russ Jandoli was beloved by his students and his graduates and always informally invited them to visit campus, make guest appearances in classes and help students and graduates with scholarship money or job connections. When Father Neil O'Connell was president, Jandoli convinced him that there should be an "Advisory Council to the President on Journalism." Father Neil went along, and the council was formed, including alumni, newspaper editors, publishers, and even some big wheels from network TV who were friends with Jandoli.

It was an honor being named, and Dr. Jandoli hoped the council could give advice to him on the future of the journalism program that he could pass onto to the president for action. At worst the council would be a think tank. At best it might come up with actionable items for the president. Just over a year following Wickenheiser's appointment, he called a luncheon meeting of the council. (Author's note: I was a member of the council then, and later was hired in 2002 by Wickenheiser as a journalism professor. At this writing, I still hold the teaching job.)

At the luncheon on campus, Wickenheiser introduced us to members of the administration of the School of Business and made a speech extolling all the lofty common goals of the journalism program and the business program. Other than investigative reporting that might send businessmen to jail, most of us on the council couldn't find any common goals with the business types.

Near the end of Wickenheiser's speech, he bore in on the target. He wanted us to give more money.

The author called that to his attention as not a valid reason for the existence of an advisory council. You could say Bob listened. The first words I ever spoke to him were probably my last, I thought. That wasn't so, as you've already found out. But it was the last meeting ever of the advisory panel. He just called it all off, and since it was officially titled an advisory council to him, there was nothing Russ Jandoli or the rest of us could do.

Dr. Don Zekan (Remember him? He was the guy who announced the university was nearly bankrupt.) served as the top financial officer and as a vice president when Wickenheiser took the presidency. In an interview, he told the author that he left because he knew he wasn't going to be rehired when his contract ran out. "Let's put it this way," he said, "Wick didn't like the way I did things. I don't think he liked me either."

University sources told the author that Dr. Wickenheiser was much more confident of the abilities of Zekan's assistant, Brenda McGee. Ms. McGee soon moved up and today is the senior vice president of finance and administration at the university, backing up Bob's choice of her in the first place.

There was always a high stress level working for Wickenheiser. The author wasn't much affected as a lowly instructor in the J/MC school. Our paths barely crossed in the 22 months I worked under him, but I watched him act up at basketball games, and listened to many speeches that I can only describe as unctuous, regardless of their topics.

As most college presidents do when they have the chance, Wickenheiser tried to load the university board of trustees with "Friends of Bob." The board was technically his boss, if not actually, and having a list of friends when in need meant he could drive through initiatives he wanted without much opposition.

This led him to make one of the decisions that still affect the financial health of the university today. It's known loosely as the "Castle deal," the purchase of land across the street from the current campus for expansion. Some call it "Wickenheiser's revenge."

One of western New York's best restaurants was opened in 1946 directly across from the east side of the Bonaventure campus. The Castle was a destination restaurant with Italian specialties so popular that it drew customers from as far away as Buffalo regularly. For a while, the Castle's owners, the Buchello family, also sold their sauces through a frozen food subsidiary. As years went by, they built a motel on the 17-acre property and a movie theater. Deaths in the family finally brought the Castle's success to an end in 1999.

The property was in two parcels, and was up for grabs at an auction in 2001. Wickenheiser wanted the property for Bonaventure, and arranged that one of the university's trustees would place a bid to get the main 13-acre parcel. He didn't want anyone to know Bona was bidding in an effort to keep the price down. The bid at $923,000 was successful. "Nobody knew St. Bonaventure was bidding, which was the best way to confuse everybody and end up getting (the property) for a nice price," Wickenheiser said after the bid worked. Shortly after, the smaller parcel of four acres was bought by the university for a figure believed in the half-million dollar range. Wickenheiser found he needed the smaller parcel to make the bigger parcel useful.

The Castle property remained a boat anchor on the university's books through 2011. The cost of mortgage and taxes each year runs to more than $120,000, and the vacant weed-infested land is an ugly visual counterpoint to the manicured campus lawns and shrubbery across Route 417. The first company Bonaventure hired to develop it didn't get anywhere attracting anyone to buy into the project. Finally, after demolishing the old restaurant and motel, COR Development pulled out in 2008 and handed a bill for demolition cost topping $200,000 to Vice President McGee. The university paid the bill.

In 2009, Wickenheiser showed the author color drawings of what he conceived would be a good use for the property, but that's as far as the land purchase has progressed since 2001. Bonaventure's 300-acre campus never needed the Castle land, and the cost of Wickenheiser's "development" idea has topped $1.5 million and still is climbing. In 2010 the university found another developer from Buffalo. A multi-million dollar "Bonaventure Square" complex of shops, apartments and restaurants is supposedly going to be built on the site.

The money spent on the Castle properties purchase is just a drop in the bucket compared to what the president's actions would cost St. Bonaventure in the years ahead.

Chapter Ten

Late in the spring of 2002, St. Bonaventure made its pitch to Jamil Terrell, offering him a scholarship to play men's basketball for van Breda Kolff. Terrell is a native of Pearson, Georgia, a small town with a population of 1805 according to the 2000 census, tucked in the southeast corner of the state. It's near nowhere, but not far from Waycross.

That same year Jamil graduated from Atkinson County High School and left his mother and three sisters to enroll in Coastal Georgia Community College in Brunswick, 91 miles to the east. The school changed its name to College of Coastal Georgia in 2008 and currently has 3200 students with a master plan calling for enrollment of 10,000.

His coach was Gerald Cox, entering his 28th year of running a competitive junior college basketball "program" in the fall of 2010. Jamil was considered a late bloomer, even by the standards of junior college recruiting, but his size at 6-8, and his speed for a big man, made him an attractive recruit for Coach Cox.

Terrell's raw strength and jumping ability soon caught the attentions of several Division One coaches, whose eyes glittered at the thought of him in their lineup, but glazed when he found out what he was taking at the college.

Terrell was enrolled in a welding program, course after course involving acetylene torches, sparks splashing metal masks, and steel neatly seamed together. It was a certificate program, teaching an enrollee the trade so he could walk out into the work world and make a living welding. Terrell was also required to take a smattering of some liberal arts courses such as

English and history. He didn't do very well in those. Ironically, he even flunked a welding course along the way.

On the basketball court it was a different story. By his second season Terrell attracted several D-1 assistants whose jobs were to do the scouting and then invite their boss to look at a prospect at the appropriate time. He was contacted, he told the NCAA later, by Eastern Kentucky, Louisville, Georgia State, Indiana State, Idaho and St. Bonaventure.

After taking a look at his academic record, bird dogs from Indiana State and Georgia State told him he would have to "redshirt" (sit out a year) before he could possibly play for them. He told the NCAA that he was recruited for Bonaventure by assistant coach Kenny Blakeney, who "said I would come in and play. Nobody said anything else."

At the same time Blakeney was pitching Bonaventure, Terrell was also being strongly recruited by Eastern Kentucky, but he told the NCAA that he picked the Allegany school because he had met the coaches there, and hadn't that kind of contact at Eastern.

Terrell's college coach had reservations about that. Jamil told the NCAA Cox asked him: " 'You go play when you get there?' I was like 'Yeah, why do you say that?' He asked if I was sure and I said 'that's what they told me.' And he said 'I thought that would be a problem.'"

At the time, the university registrar, Barbara Russell, had to deal with Terrell's academic record. It basically was her job to determine whether a student transferring into Bonaventure had enough credits to qualify for the university. She was involved with that only, not with any NCAA eligibility to play sports.

It seems a bit confusing. But essentially, Terrell could have been admitted as a transfer student without coming close to immediate eligibility as a varsity athlete. She said she dealt with Kort Wickenheiser when it came time to evaluate Terrell's academic standing. She told the internal investigation committee Wickenheiser was close to bullying her to get Terrell admitted. "I guess I felt some pressure," she said.

Rich Hilliard was a former NCAA official hired to lead the ultimate Bona internal committee inquiry He asked her: "OK, and was that message from Kort consistent with what you were getting from Dr. Wickenheiser?"

Russell: "Yes."

Hilliard: "Was Dr. Wickenheiser reminding you repeatedly?"

Russell: "...the primary, primary, primary cause of the phone calls between me and Dr. Wickenheiser was if this degree was equivalent to an associate's."

She explained that "the registrar evaluates the transcript taking each course from another school and evaluates it to a Bonaventure course. I sent this to the Academic Department and it was sent back with a note on it:' Are you kidding?' so, no, I wasn't 100 per cent comfortable bringing in welding classes."

She said she was encouraged by the coaches and the president to accept enough of Terrell's courses so that he met Bonaventure's requirements for transfer of at least 50 per cent completed course work towards a bachelor's degree.

Russell told the committee Dr. Wickeheiser wanted her to get a letter from her opposite at Coastal Georgia indicating Terrell was a qualified student. "He wanted me to get a letter, but told me that the one thing he didn't want to see in writing that his academic work was not equivalent (to an associate's degree.)"

Wickenheiser badgered Russell through the spring semester right up to graduation, pushing to make sure a letter arrived that might help Terrell qualify to the NCAA, and a letter that didn't mention at all that he didn't qualify, a back-handed way to solve the problem. Under pressure from the big boss, Russell begged off that she was too busy with graduation duties to effect getting a letter.

"If you ever talked to Dr. Wickenheiser, you know you don't say much, you listen a lot," she told the committee.

Meanwhile, Barbara Questa, the athletics department expert on eligibility issues, had been examining Terrell's record and had checked with the A-10 and the NCAA about the player. Strangely, the NCAA never responded to the data she sent, but an A-10 official told her that in all likelihood Terrell was ineligible.

Questa met with Kort Wickenheiser privately, and she said he agreed that his recruit was ineligible to play.

If you put the three together, you have the registrar (Russell), the NCAA compliance officer (Questa) and a coach (Kort W.) in agreement that Terrell would not be able to take the court in the fall.

Enter Gothard Lane, the athletic director and vice president. He had been at odds with President Wickenheiser for months. "In September 2001, President Wickenheiser started to complain about the quality of work by Steve Mest, my assistant athletics director of media relations," said Lane.

"He (President Wickenheiser) was upset at Mr. Mest's articles from the preseason European trip of the men's basketball team. He went on to state that Mr. Mest's last three (out of six) articles were better and President

Wickenheiser attributed that to his sense that his son Kort, an assistant basketball coach, must have helped Mr. Mest write the articles."

"The thing was he (van Breda Kolff) knew he had a back door to the
president and I was aware of that and I figured that, you know, that was the
issue. Every once in a while, I'd get called into the president's office and he'd
start complaining that there were certain people in my department who
weren't being supportive of basketball," Lane recalled.

In January of 2002 the president called Lane into his office, and his first
words were orders to fire Steve Mest, Barbara Questa, and a student assistant named Greg Kennedy who was a commentator on Bona radio game
broadcasts.

Lane's reaction: "I said, 'well Doc, you can't quite do this in the middle of
the season. We only had one SID and if we get rid of Steve, there's nobody
to take care of the sport. Barb Questa is doing nothing wrong and Greg Kennedy, what's the poor guy on the radio done?' I said, let me work on it. So I
went back and tried to schmooze everybody and he calls me and says later:
'They're gone. I want them fired today.' I said again, ' I can't do it Doc. It's the
wrong time of the year and they haven't done anything wrong.'"

Lane went back to his Reilly Center office and called in Kennedy, who
apparently had upset the coaching staff or van Breda Kolff with some mildly
critical remarks on a game broadcast. He relieved Kennedy of his on-air
duties and assigned him to other jobs in the department. But he took no
action on the other two staff members.

A month later Wickenheiser repeated his firing order for Mest and
Questa. Again Lane held off the president, pointing out that there would be
no media relations person for the last month of the season if Mest was fired.
Lane had fought off the president again, but it was to cost him dearly.

Lane decided to take away Questa's day-to-day contact with the men's
basketball program to keep the presidential pressure off her back, and
assign that to Steve Campbell, another assistant athletics director. Questa
would still be in charge of compliance to NCAA regulations, but Campbell
would be the intermediary between her and the coaching staff.

Van Breda Kolff also had a demand of his own. He wanted to control the
finances of the men's basketball program.

Ordinarily a school's total athletic budget is under the administration
and control of its athletic director. That sentence applies to small colleges
in Divisions Two and Three of the NCAA. With the steady move towards athletic "programs" that are really big business, coaches in many Division One
schools demand and receive financial control over their sport—football or
basketball. With million-dollar-plus salaries and a dozens of assistants and

flunkies, college football and basketball coaches are the new royalty in America's part of the sporting world.

They can move around. They can threaten to leave. They can become icons like Bear Bryant, or idols with clay feet like Bobby Knght, Rick Pitino and John Calapari. They are an attraction in their own right. Pete Carroll at Southern California parlayed the golden boy image into millions when he was the head football coach of the Trojans.

In some cases the football or the basketball coach is literally more powerful than the university president. The Higher Education Chronicle reported in 2010 that some chancellors and presidents of state schools were afraid to exercise any kind of authority over sports programs like football and basketball because they might lose their jobs. Legislators who were graduates or supporter of good old State U—or maybe even played in the annual Old Rusty Washtub game against A & M– had the power to take down a university president. And many are the presidents who felt the power at times.

The same thing goes at private schools. No one has a bigger and more emotional fan base than Notre Dame. The football team's record and the success of its coaches is paramount to alumni and most of the university's trustees. Without football, ND would just be another Catholic college with a pretty campus. It may be a fine academic institution, but its public image is all about football.

Bob Wickenheiser told the author that he wanted St. Bonaventure to become a school like Villanova or Boston College. To do that, he said all elements of the university had to improve, and that included basketball. Wickenheiser had joined Bona at the end of some of worst basketball the school had ever suffered through. Even Jim Baron only scraped through with just above a .500 record, so Wickenheiser's hiring of van Breda Kolff at the highest salary ever paid a Bona employee or coach was his way of starting a return to what he hoped would be national prominence.

St. Bonaventure is no Villanova or Boston College, and never will be. It's a rural school in a rural corner of New York. Villanova has nearly 11,000 students on its Philadelphia campus, and Boston College has more than 9000 undergraduates. St. Bonaventure has 2000 most years.

Through either his son, Kort, or from the head coach himself, the president kept getting complaints that the basketball budget wasn't be handled correctly under Gothard Lane. The athletic director had this evaluation of VBK as a coach and an employee: "A very good bench coach, court coach, everybody said. But a lot of basketball coaches are a little strange. They're all very hyper, very focused on what they're doing. They can be tough to deal with.

"The budget is always an issue because they always want more. But for the most part, I was able to structure it for them to accomplish most of the things they wanted to do as far as recruiting, how they traveled, and all that kind of thing," he said. Lane was being put in a corner by the fall of 2002. Either he allow van Breda Kolff to run his own budget or Lane would lose all oversight on men's basketball, Wickenheiser told him.

"It was standard operating procedure for either Karen Hill, director of business operations for the athletic department or I to provide oversight for all expenditures for each of our cost centers so that we would not overspend the budget or violate any A-10 or NCAA rules stemming from improper purchases, but I was getting email after email from Wickenheiser and VP for Finance Brenda McGee Snow telling me to turn over control of the budget without oversight to the basketball office" Lane said.

Not anymore. Instead Bob and Kort Wickenheiser were remaking the department under Gothard's nose. He had already warned them about Terrell in the spring.

Chapter Eleven

There weren't too many people in the spring of 2002 who thought that Jamil Terrell would be eligible to play college basketball for St. Bonaventure in the fall, even his junior college coach.

Julie Steinke was an assistant athletics director charged with riding herd on the academic performance of all of those on Bona varsity teams. Her heaviest remedial work load came from members of the men's basketball team, but that wasn't unusual at D-1 schools without varsity football programs.

SBU's registrar Barbara Russell's put the president's order aside by saying that she was too busy with the upcoming graduation to continue to contact the registrar at Coastal Georgia Community College. At Lane's direction, Steinke had written Coastal Georgia. Her letter asked for an evaluation of Jamil's academic record to find out if it was equivalent to an associate's. She asked that a copy of the reply be sent to Russell. Remember that Russell, the university registrar, had been bullied by Dr. Wickenheiser ever since Jamil Terrell came onto Bona's basketball radar. Wickenheiser kept calling Russell, urging her to get a letter from Georgia, but only one that said Terrell was holding the equivalent of an associates degree. The letter that Lane had asked for finally came and it said he wasn't equivalent. When Russell got it, she filed it.

Steinke was called by Gerald Cox, the Coastal Georgia coach. "He told me he was looking for some information about Jamil," she said to members of the internal investigation committee. "And whether we would be able to certify him. He wanted to know if that was going to happen, if not, because he had some other places that Jamil was looking at going, and he wanted to make sure that Jamil wasn't going to get screwed over."

"Screwed over" is a pithy description for what happens to many high school and junior college basketball players who are recruited to play at the D-1 level. They are pretty much pieces of basketball meat, prodded by coaches to stay eligible and take the easiest courses just so they can play for the greater glory and financial recompense of the coach.

Some coaches and "programs" are sleazier than others, admitting "student athletes" who will never be close to being a student in college, and couldn't count to double figures even if that's their scoring average. The colleges use the players, even when they're being recruited. They come to campuses for "official visits" and are given tryouts.

Sometimes they leave thinking they might get a scholarship offer. This might happen, though not if a better prospect at their position comes to campus a few days later. The whole education scenario is reversed for big-time college sports A normal applicant to a university is admitted based on grades, SAT's and maybe an essay.

Basketball and football players are admitted based on athletic ability, and in many cases, with the kind of grades and SAT's that would be laughed at by the college's admissions office if the player was trying to get in as a normal student. The double standard feeds the "program" in basketball or football, or both.

Coach Cox at Coastal Georgia knew there were at least two other schools willing to take Terrell as a "student athlete," two that Terrell later mentioned in his testimony to the NCAA.

The whole Terrell issue was front and center in Gothard Lane's concerns in May of 2002. Lane recalled: "It wasn't a basketball issue. It was an academic issue. So we wrote the letter and so in two days, this is like the 5th of May, and in a day we get it back, saying they did not consider the certificate in technical welding to be equivalent to an associate degree. So immediately I email Bob Wickenheiser saying that Coastal Georgia had finally spoken and that it was not equivalent, so we couldn't recruit the kid. And within the hour I walked over to van Breda Kolff and met with him personally and said 'Forget about Jamil. Go find another big man.'

"Maybe they just were recruiting somebody they hoped would meet NCAA standards, one way or the other. But just that he needed to forget about the kid and go find somebody else. So I thought that was the end of it. That was a Wednesday or a Thursday.

"The very next week I get a call from the president and was told to come over to the president's office. You know, not knowing what it's all about, I go over and I walk in and van Breda Kolff is in the office with Bob and they want to talk about Jamil Terrell. Bob starts off by saying, 'This kid is eligible and we're going to be declaring him eligible.' Now you've got to realize that we're dealing with two different issues here. One is any school can admit anyone they wish. But that doesn't mean the person would be eligible according to NCAA rules.

"Bob always had the authority to do that and so he did. So I'm saying, ' Sure you can take the kid, you can admit him but he can't play and he's going to have to red shirt. He's probably not eligible. We'd have to look into that.' So in his opinion, the certificate of welding is equivalent to an associate degree. And I said, 'Doc, we just got that letter back last week saying that it isn't and there is no way we can do this.' This went on for about twenty minutes and he keeps beating this dog. And Jan was there and was saying he agreed with Bob, the kid was eligible and so forth. And I said, ' Look, if you guys go forward with this, people will know about this kid, sooner or later somebody is going to challenge it and if you're wrong, there's going to be a big price to pay.' And that's when Jan said, ' Hey, other schools don't turn other schools in '"

Van Breda Kolff was correct, at least in this case. I found out that though many coaches in the east knew of Terrell's situation and talked about Bonaventure taking on a player who probably was ineligible, no coach or athletic department ever reported this to the NCAA or the A-10.

In a lengthy interview in 2008, Bob Wickenheiser told the author that he relied on Barbara Russell, the university registrar, to help him determine if Terrell was eligible. "I trusted her completely and when I called her I always knew I'd get a straight answer," he said. "So before the meeting that I'd set up with Gothard and Jan, I called over to her and asked a number of questions.

"One, is this student different from other students we had accepted? And she said, 'yes and no'. I said just tell me. She said, 'He's very much like any student we've accepted from Alfred and other two-year colleges where the kind of technology they've studied is different from what we would have them do at Bonaventure and sometimes they won't get all the credit they'd like. But they get sufficient.' I said, 'Well, you've seen Jamil's material. What is your opinion and she said 'All I know is he is very much like others we've taken from Alfred .' Now that was that conversation. I swear to God. I wish I'd taped it. Because people changed and that's how I know something was happening from the top down because nothing changes people more than fear. And Barb would never have said something other later, which she did at the meeting, or the hearing with the NCAA. I talked to Barb. (I)... had the meeting with her."

Wickenheiser's recall of the meeting with his AD and his coach varies from Lane's and places the issue as a fight between those two.

"You would hope that Gothard would do this on his own." The president said. "Let them fight it out. They came to no agreement after about an hour and 15 minutes and I said, 'Okay, Gothard, I've reviewed the case. I've asked our admissions director who has been there for a long time what this student was like, and if we'd taken students like him before particularly from Alfred. I said apparently what he's taken and what we're accrediting is not different from what was done with other students from there. So, I said, I don't have any reason to say you shouldn't take the student.' And underneath I believe he was still fighting with Jan."

Van Breda Kolff had this to say in his NCAA testimony: "Every conversation I had with Dr. Wickeheiser dealt with dysfunctional family…He tried to be the mediator between the basketball office and the athletics administration. It was amazing that on a daily basis, the arguments, over other so many unrelated things, that it was non-stop…in those meetings I had with the president and the athletics director I was always caught between a rock and a hard place because the president is the CEO.

"He's the one I have to answer to and agree with, yet my ultimate boss— my reporting boss—is the athletics director. I'm caught with who I am supposed to side with."

Wickenheiser was defining the Terrell issue as a dispute between Lane and van Breda Kolff, while they both were putting it more on the president's lap. The president liked to be in direct charge of things in men's basketball, or at least someone else named Wickenheiser liked to have the whip hand in the sport.

Kort Wickenheiser denied that he knew anything about the letter from Coastal Georgia that had been received by Bonaventure. He was asked by Hilliard in the university investigation: "Did you talk to your father about how Jamil Terrell became eligible?" His answer was: No."

President Wickenheiser, Lane said, " had another vested interest besides being an avid basketball fan. He wanted his son to be coaching at Duke, like tomorrow. And he was very supportive of his kid. Then in some of my conversations and interviews with van Breda Kolff, as I remember now, he said that he thought that eventually Bob would get rid of him and make Kort the coach."

Both van Breda Kolff and Lane knew that from the day Kort Wickenheiser was hired, his father would not only have more interest (if that's possible) in basketball, and his son would have his own private pipeline into the president's office. That may have seemed attractive to van Breda Kolff in the beginning. When he wanted something, he went to Kort, and Kort went to Dad. As things progressed, he now had to be concerned with two Wickenheisers looking over his shoulder, not just one.

Lane also received feedback from the university's business office that Kort was "throwing his name" around. Lane called Kort into his office and told him that he had to stop and he has a choice to make. He could be known on campus as an adult assistant basketball coach or as "the president's little boy."

Kort said when he signed Terrell to the NCAA's national letter of intent (in effect it binds a player to a school, and the school to the player) he did so at van Breda Kolff's order. Technically, of course, the head coach does decide the players to be signed to national leters of intent, but van Breda Kolff knew from the spring of 2002 that Jamil Terrell was likely a non-qualifier. He went ahead nonetheless, comforted by Kort's assurances that his dad would declare Jamil eligible.

After the meeting with the president and the coach, Lane was not about to give up trying to convince President Wickenheiser that Terrell was ineligible.

The Father: Dr. Robert J. Wickenheiser
President, St. Bonaventure University.

The Son: Kort Wickenheiser
Assistant Men's Basketball Coach.

The Coach: Jan van Breda Kolff
Target—The Sweet Sixteen.

The Player: Jamil Terrell
Used as a pawn.

The AD: Gothard Lane
He protested to no avail.

The Star: Marques Green
A leader of the walkout.

The Pro: J.R. Bremer
Got a free ride.

Chapter Twelve

A few weeks later Lane attended a meeting with the university's board of trustees, and sought out Jim Gould, a 1980 Bona graduate who was chairman of the trustees committee on athletics.

"Jim, I need your help," Lane said. "Bob wants to find this kid's eligible and he, in my opinion, is not eligible. Can you give me some advice? He says 'yeah, he's the president and the president's the president, so presidents do what presidents want to do. Send me an email or write me a note explaining everything so he has it on paper.' So I decided to do it by email because I wanted an electronic copy of it."

The email from Lane to Wickenheiser, (with a copy to Gould) began: "I know that we talked about this before, but I believe we have a problem that we need to talk about again. You pay me to keep St. Bonaventure out of trouble when it comes to athletics and that is what I am trying to do.

"The more I think about Jamil's eligibility situation the more I am convinced that we cannot unilaterally declare him eligible to compete this year. Coastal Georgia has stated that under their academic structure that his 'certificate' is not equivalent to an associate degree. In my opinion, if we declare him eligible, we leave ourselves open to a possible NCAA violation. I do not believe we can ignore their institutional stance without putting ourselves in possible jeopardy."

Lane's email went on to say that Terrell should be "redshirted" for the coming season, meaning he would not be able to play, but could practice with the team. Or better yet, the email said, Bonaventure should petition the NCAA to determine his eligibility. Lane didn't question whether Bona could admit Terrell, and that was a good thing, as he was already enrolled for two summer school classes, back-to-back five-week sessions in Spanish 101 and 102 (the beginner level in college.)

The president second-guessed himself in that 2008 interview: "And what I should have written back in an email was: ' You're the AD. Make the damn decision and stand by it. I'll stand by you. And if you're wrong, you'll have to admit it. We all make mistakes.' That is what I should have written. But I was so bloody mad at Gothard for dragging this thing on. This was like the sixth week. How many weeks do you want to talk to the president and ask if a basketball player should come in? It's ridiculous.

"So I let all my stuff hang out and I wrote an email back saying you've yet to show me anything that says he's different from anyone else that Barb Russell talked about and then I outlined and I'm sure you've seen that memo that I sent. It came out later. I had no problem answering that. I said, of course I turned to my son for help. While I know what the NCAA rule book says as it applies to presidents, I certainly don't know how it applies to coaches. So I needed some help. So, Kort said you want to look at these, this article and this, so I said okay, thanks, whatever and that's what made me write the letter. It was pretty specific."

That's not exactly what he told the NCAA when he testified in its investigation. The first time President Wickenheiser met with the committee he said he wrote the response email to Lane that justified his decision to declare Terrell eligible, with some help from his son Kort on certain points.

When Lane received the president's email, he didn't give up. He went back to trustee Gould. "I just knew something was wrong because I knew Bob didn't have an NCAA manual," he said.

"Somebody obviously helped him with it. But anyway, in the end he says he's eligible and we're going to certify the kid eligible. So I get back to Jim Gould and telling him this is what happened and sending him copies of the email and he forwards it to Bill Swan, (chairman of the university board of trustees) because I'm saying that Bob is wrong. Bob is the president and Bob can do what he wants because he's got the most power.

"As all of this is going on, we had an end-of-the-year dinner for the vice presidents and key people over at Bob's house, and in walked Bob. I walk over to him and say, "Bob I got your email. You're wrong. If we do this...'

"He gets mad at me and says, 'Look I don't want to hear about this anymore. You're either on the bus or off the bus. You're going to do this or else.' So okay, I just walk away. In the meantime Gould gets back to me and he says he's going to forward it by email to Swan. So the next thing I know is, a week later Swan calls me."

Bill Swan was close to the president. At least, that's how it appeared to the Bonaventure community. It was rumored that he was Wickenheiser's personal choice to be named the chairman of the trustees' board. Swan was certainly a basketball buddy of the president. He often sat next to him at Reilly Center games, and had served as the Brown Indian symbol mascot while an undergraduate at Bonaventure.

Swan had risen from relative obscurity to head what had been a small local bank in the area northeast of Buffalo to what was becoming a regional banking power. He was a rah-rah alumnus of Bona, and was quick to show friends that he carried a printed list of Franciscan principles in his suit coat pocket. Tall and intense, Swan would play the tragic role in the story a few months later.

Lane said Swan called him a few days later. Lane recalled Swan's words: "Look, I read both emails. I read your email to Bob saying he can't do it and I read Bob's email back to you saying he could do it and his email is very persuasive and I'm siding with Bob. And if he's wrong, it's going to be on Bob's shoulders."

In his testimony before the internal investigation committee and the NCAA, Swan later observed: "Frankly, I felt that this was time to back off, and at that point I didn't want to call Bob, to challenge his authority or our confidence in him, because we had confidence. If you read the thing (president's email) it sounds like he knew what he was talking about."

Swan said neither he nor Gould talked to Wickenheiser about the email exchange between the president and Lane, or about Jamil Terrell. Swan testified that he "had too many things on his plate" at the time he was briefed on the whole matter to take it any further. Lane said "Bill Swan was not willing to buck Wickenheiser.."

It was a mistake that cost the university in a myriad of ways, and ultimately may have cost Swan his life.

Ironically, Wickenheiser was so driven by whatever force that he treasured—being the boss or being right—that he turned to his son Kort, an assistant basketball coach, for a determination on Terrill. Perhaps he was blinded by family ties, by his hopes for his son's career, by his fanaticism for the sport, that he had Kort write the email finally received by Lane, and seen by Gould and Swan.

President Wickenheiser's response to Lane's email was not only written by his son Kort, but the president passed it off as HIS (emphasis from author) creation, according to his first testimony to the NCAA. Lane was convinced the email hadn't been written by the president, and so were investigators.

After the NCAA asked Lane for his help with reviewing the SBU email database, Lane dug up emails between the president and his son, and found the one sent to Lane was nearly identical to one prepared for the president by his son.

Wickenheiser, the father, lied in his first testimony, and later admitted to the mistruth. But that was only after the walls came tumbling down on his career, and the university was soiled.

But much more was to happen before the whole story broke in February of 2003. Lane had formally brought the Terrill matter to the president while he was being recruited in the spring of 2002, and by summer had been rebuffed and frustrated by Wickenheiser, Gould and Swan.

Gothard Lane was in a terrible spot. He not only had told the boss that the boss was wrong, he had told the boss's boss—Swan—that he was wrong. The president was not one to take criticism or disagreement lightly. Lane knew he was probably going to be separated from his job when his current contract ran out in 2003.

Chapter Thirteen

The basketball season ahead showed promise for Bonaventure. It would be van Breda Kolff's second recruiting class, though he hardly had control of the player recruiting for his first team, joining Bona in April of 2001.

His team was undersized as of the spring of 2002. Returning were the flashy Marques Green, another of the undersized quick guards that Bona seemed to attract, and Mike Gansey, a 6-4 swingman who played with an intensity seldom matched by anyone else on the court. Gansey wasn't a great shooter, but a good streak shooter, and rebounded far better than his size would predict. The A-10 would be difficult for Bona once again. Considered to be about the fifth or sixth best conference in the country, the A-10 was made up then of big schools compared to Bonaventure's 2000-student enrollment. Temple under Coach John Chaney was a national power most seasons. Massachusetts had produced Julius Erving in the past, and the UMass teams were usually strong.

Add Jamil Terrell to the mix. The 6-8 forward was the player van Breda Kolff wanted to bring muscle and rebounding to a team that was strong in fancy play with Green and Prado, a team whose best clutch rebounder was Gansey. A big man who could play would be enough to make Bona competitive in the A-10. Van Breda Kolff came east from Pepperdine, it was reported, to be closer to his family. There were no illusions among long-time fans or members of the athletic administration about Jan. Bonaventure was just a way station for the coach. Then that's usually the way it is today at most D-1 schools except the elite jobs like Kentucky, Duke and North Carolina. A coach wins for a while and gets hired a step up to a more elite school in a more elite conference, and makes more money when he does so.

According to federal income tax returns, van Breda Kolff was making $325,000 annually as the Bona coach, plus about another $25,000 in benefits. Small change, it was, compared to even some other salaries in the A-10. St. Joseph's, a school not much bigger than Bonaventure, pays its coach Phil Martelli in the neighborhood of $800,000 a year, according to one of the school's recent tax returns. The president of St. Bonaventure made $130,000, plus benefits, the first year van Breda Kolff was the coach.

One of the nation's most successful coaches at job jumping ever upward is John Beilein, the current Michigan coach, who is said to at least top a million dollars a year, Beilein started at Division Two Lemoyne College, moved up to Canisius, then to Richmond in the A-10, onward to West Virginia, and ultimately to Michigan. He had success each place, and his West Virginia team in 2006 nearly pulled off a Cinderella victory in the NCAA tournament, thanks in part to a thrilling tournament performance by none other than Mike Gansey. More about that later on.

In summer school 2002, Terrell took basic Spanish courses back-to-back, five weeks in 101, and five weeks in 102. He took them both from Dr. Leigh Simone, an alumna of Bonaventure and an assistant professor of modern languages. Dr. Simone told the investigating committee that she was often in contact with Steinke, the assistant AD who was the academic "coach" for Bona athletes.

That was largely because every Bona student in the School of Arts and Sciences has a language requirement, and many choose Spanish as their language to study. Terrell was placed in Spanish, but it's not clear who advised him to take it. He passed both summer courses and was placed in the next logical course, Spanish 201, for the fall semester. Dr. Simone was again to be his teacher. Terrell told investigators that Dr. Simone was "a great teacher."

Steinke served as Terrell's academic coach that summer, and continued in the fall when Jamil was enrolled for three courses in sociology (his major) and the Spanish course. That would give him 12 credit hours, the minimum required at Bonaventure to be considered a full-time student. It's not unusual for varsity athletes to take only 12 hours, particularly men's and women's basketball players who are required to play in 25 games or so, plus post-season tournaments. They travel so frequently that they miss classes and have to make up assignments. Some Bonaventure professors don't allow for students missing classes for sports, and even though the university asks profs to cut the athletes some slack, a few just won't do it.

Needless to say, those professors seldom find basketball players enrolled in their classes. Steinke's job includes counseling athletes on all the possible situations that might arise in the teachers they pick or don't pick for a course.

Some college professors who are opposed to big-time sports programs on a campus go out of their way to stick it to a student-athlete. Others are known to be "friendly" to athletes, and some become much too friendly. A few years ago, Auburn University was rocked by a scandal involving a prof who was signing up football players for "independent study" and doling out A grades to all, though they had almost no academic requirements to get the grades.

Steinke knew about all there was to know regarding the "easy" and the "tough" professors in the small university that currently has about 200 faculty members. The sociology major had traditionally been the major of choice for men's basketball players. Other athletes in other D-1 sports at the school are spread throughout all its courses of study.

Sometimes professors, including the author, are surprised by the sense of commitment from varsity athletes, particularly women. To play a D-1 sport such as basketball, with 20 practice hours and games a week, plus travel, a student must superbly organize his or her life to succeed at both. And many do, sacrificing neither their sport nor their education.

But at Bonaventure, as many schools, the grade point average (GPA) of the men's basketball team is usually the lowest among all the sports teams. That's even with those walk on's who boost the GPA of the basketball team.

Kort Wickenheiser was the coach in charge of the "big men" on van Breda Kolff's roster. He decided that he was going to be in charge of Terrell off the court too. Jamil was struggling in Dr. Simone's Spanish 201 class but he believed he had a good chance of passing, he told investigators. "After practice he calls me over and tells me that he dropped me out of the Spanish class and I didn't know anything about it...We didn't go over if I wanted to (sic) get dropped out. I was mad that he dropped me out of the class so I really just walked away...and didn't want to talk to him about it." Terrell said. "I could have passed the class. I didn't understand."

Neither did Dr. Simone. "This kid wanted to take the final exam," she testified. "He wanted to prove himself. He was not a good student but he really worked hard." She said Terrell came to me and told me he couldn't take the final because his coach had withdrawn him from the course.

Ordinary withdrawal procedure at Bonaventure calls for the signed approval of both the professor teaching the course, and the academic adviser of the student who's withdrawing. Dr. Simone said she was completely bypassed by the withdrawal in Terrell's case. She had suggested that Terrell take an incomplete grade in the course, which is allowed and within her power to grant. That way, Terrell could come back to campus after the semester break with plenty of time to study for the final.

An incomplete is just that, failure to complete a course's requirements. They are often granted. But Terrell wasn't going to get an incomplete in that Spanish course, even though he wanted to take the exam at the time Dr. Simone set for him, January 13, 2002.

Instead he was taken out of the course by Kort Wickenheiser with his father's active cooperation. In fact, if the president hadn't stepped in, there would have been no withdrawal, the grade that means what it says: you're out of the course with no credit.

Kort Wickenheiser thought that was the best thing for the basketball team, and the hell with the student. He reasoned that Terrell would probably flunk Spanish 201, with the result that his grade point average would drop below 2.0, the magic basic "C" grade. If so, Terrell would have been put on what Bonaventure calls "academic restoration," a classy name for a kind of part time academic jail.

That's because those students on academic restoration are not allowed to miss ANY (author's emphasis) classes. That would mean Terrell wouldn't be able to travel to any road games in the second semester, when Bona played its entire A-10 schedule and the conference tournament. He was the best big man on the team, and vital to its conference success.

So Kort Wickenheiser arranged a "W" in the Spanish course. The formal request came in an email from Julie Steinke, at Kort's behest. It went to the acting registrar, Heather Jackson, who kicked it upstairs where it first took a bad bounce.

To get it done, President Wickenheiser had to apply muscle on the university provost, the highest academic administrator, Frank E. "Skip" Saal. He preferred being called Skip, though he was full-blown academic with the customary Ph.D. and the title of vice president for academic affairs.

Saal, a short dark-haired man with thick glasses, later told investigators that he was turning down the request for a Terrell withdrawal until his boss intervened. "In the context of my on-going crusade to emphasize and raise our standards for academic standards," he testified, he was not allowing the withdrawal. It was past the posted deadline for withdrawals, far beyond the date in the first semester by which all withdrawals were allowed.

Saal had been on the job less than two years, when the boss called him at home the night of January 5, 2002 and asked him to allow the "W" grade for Terrell. "Dr. Wickenheiser asked me to consider delaying strict enforcement of the withdrawal date deadline until such time as all SBU students, including student athletes, could be fully informed that this deadline would henceforth be strictly enforced," he said.

The heat was on Saal. His boss wanted him to let the W stand based on some arcane interpretation of his that the withdrawal date hadn't been strictly enforced in the past. In fact, there was another student seeking a withdrawal from a course at the same time as Terrell. But that student at least had received endorsement from his professor backing up the request.

Dr. Simone wasn't involved at all in the Terrell request. She didn't even know about it. She had given Terrell an "I"—an incomplete—with the belief he would take his 201 final on Jan. 13.

Saal told the investigators "a grade change originates with a faculty member, proceeds through the chair, typically through a chair and a dean. And ultimately gets to me." That hadn't happened at all. Leigh Simone hadn't any part in the matter, and she was Terrell's professor. Dr. Simone told investigators "it was a little disconcerting. But my response, my reaction is… can it be done?" She raised her right hand to swear she didn't know a thing about the W in advance, noting, "there is no bible" to the investigators.

Chapter Fourteen

This may be a good time to talk about the people who tried to track down what happened and how. After the scandal broke, the university trustees appointed an internal investigation group called the Basketball Review Committee, consisting of members of the Bonaventure faculty and administration, and outside counsel, the previously identified Hilliard, a partner in the Indianapolis law firm of Ice Miller, a very expensive (for Bonaventure) firm that listed dealing with the NCAA as one of its specialties. Hilliard was former director of enforcement for the NCAA and served as independent counsel charged with early fact finding.

Later there was an official NCAA investigation, with Hilliard involved as the university representative, and a Pittsburgh lawyer, Jack McGinley, serving as one of the main questioners of the various witnesses. McGinley was, and is, a member of the Bonaventure Board of Trustees, and approached the job almost as a kindly prosecutor if there can be such a description.

The committee makeup stayed the same, but with the addition by phone of an NCAA representative named Jeff Higgins. Some of the testimony contained in this book was given to the internal Basketball Review Committee before Higgins joined the group, and some after he was involved. None of the testimony was sworn, but taken down by a notary public.

As they found out, there were two major violations by the president, not just one.

Jamil Terrell must have felt like he was being slapped around by life when Kort Wickenheiser told him he was withdrawn from Dr. Simone's Spanish 201 course, just after the professor informed him he would be given an incomplete and allowed to take the final just after the mid-year semester break. "I was studying hard," he told the committee.

His team had a long plane ride back from an early December game against Davidson, and Julie Steinke had taken the trip to help any player who needed academic support, particularly Jamil. "(We) were on the plane studying Spanish with flash cards," he said, "studying vocabulary and everything, and now—I mean—it comes up that it didn't even count, all of that studying, for that class."

Julie Steinke said the flash card work helped, Jamil had two quizzes and she recalled that "he got a 95 and a 100." She said Jamil told her he definitely wanted to take the final.

Dr. Simone also wanted him to take the final. "He was not a good student, but he worked hard," she testified. When Kort Wickenheiser told Jamil that he had been withdrawn from the course by his coach, others who were there say the young player stormed off the court and left practice.

Dr. Simone was of a mind to complain herself, but pulled back when she realized that it wasn't a fight she could win, a fight against Skip Saal, and more importantly, Bob Wickenheiser. "They said there's been a precedent. Students are allowed to make grade changes. I was not. I did not institute the grade change. I have to respect it. OK, out of my hands," she said.

Wickenheiser still passes the buck on the grade change issue. He told the author: "I was incensed with the charge and more than incensed, hurt. I have to say hurt when they found me guilty of that. First of all, there had never been a policy like it on the books. In other words, the choice a student has when it gets to a certain point as to whether he takes a pass/fail or he extends when he's going to take the course or close it out or a number of other considerations.

"First of all," he said, " I have never changed a grade of anyone in my life. I should say the second accusation was that your son asked you to and I said 'not at all.' I said and it really bothered me, that probably hurting me more than anything. I am an academician and I live for academics. I believe in the integrity of our teaching. Why would I do anything to jeopardize what I believe in? They accused me of stepping in and trying to say how a person's grade was or was not reported."

Who gets Wickenheiser's buck pass? Skip Saal, that's who. And he deserved at least part of it.

Saal told interviewers about the phone call to his home on a Sunday night by President Wickenheiser who told him that Coach Kort Wickenheiser had found "a difficulty…a misunderstanding" about whether a basketball player (Terrell) could withdraw from a course. The president wanted Saal to check out his withdrawal procedures and how they were being applied so his son could get Terrell a withdrawal from Dr. Simone's course. "I will confess to you that the fact the request came from the president made me uncomfortable," Saal said.

But Saal soldiered on despite some misgivings. "This request was a bit out of character given the obvious connection with his son, made me uncomfortable, but I waived my discomfort as I stayed with what I felt was in the best interest of the kids and made that decision. But I made that decision. I want to be real clear about that."

The top academic official in the university allows a basketball player to get special treatment through the intercession of the president and the president's coach son, and he takes credit for it.

"The president did not say 'do this or you're fired.' He did not say you got to do this. He did not bully or intimidate," Saal said.

So far we haven't heard Saal refer to Dr. Simone, and her role. Yet in his testimony Saal was firm about a professor's role in allowing a withdrawal. "The procedure, as I understand it is that a grade change originates with a faculty member, proceeds through a chair, typically through a chair and a dean, and ultimately gets to me," he said.

Saal had never talked to Dr. Simone about the Terrell case, but left her in the lurch when her plan was to give the young man an incomplete so he would have a chance to pass a belated final exam.

With no formal or informal evidence that Simone backed a withdrawal, Saal still told the investigators: "I believe Mr. Terrell's request to withdraw from a course after the deadline enjoyed the support of both the course instructor and the athletics department."

According to the Bonaventure committee interview of Barbara Questa, and Lane, the only meeting between Saal, Barbara Questa and Julie Steinke of the athletics department was much later. "He talks in his interview that he received assurance from Questa and Steinke that changing the grade would not violate an NCAA rule. He never met with Questa and Steinke until February 10, 2003. That was over a month after he changed the grade," Lane said.

Trustee Jim Gould told the university he had a phone conversation with Saal who told him Terrell "has to have a degree that is equivalent, and he doesn't have a degree that is equivalent." Gould said he asked Saal if Terrell had enough course work to be eligible. "Not even close," was Saal's reply, according to Gould.

Funny thing: Terrell had not asked to withdraw and Dr. Simone hadn't asked either, only the athletics department. Saal went against every university procedure after he got the phone call from President Wickenheiser.

When the internal committee submitted its report later in the spring of 2003, Saal was criticized for his role that we just outlined. He then hoisted himself on his own petard with a letter on April 17, 2003 to McGinley, the committee chairman. Saal's letter said he had received an email from Julie Steinke, the assistant athletic director saying Ms. Steinke had talked to Simone about Terrell dropping the course. "This message indicated quite clearly to me that the instructor of the course had in fact offered consent to the proposed grade change, and that the change of grade clearly did involve the instructor of the course."

Remember that Dr. Simone had testified she knew nothing about the grade change until confronted with the fait accompli. Saal didn't follow any of the procedures he had said were customary university policy; made a decision on his own, and never checked with any dean or instructor before allowing the grade to be changed, let alone concerned himself with what Terrell really wanted to do: take the test and pass.

Jamil Terrell was merely a pawn, a useful basketball player, through the actions of a coach, a university president and its top academic officer. It seems nobody gave a damn about him as a student except Dr. Simone who was trying hard to help him through Spanish 201. And she was cut off at the pass by the Wickenheiser cabal.

When Gothard Lane learned of the manipulation of Terrell's grade, he was furious.

He immediately went to Barb Questa about the change on Feb. 12, 2003, telling her that it was an NCAA violation. Lane contacted Jim Gould, the board of trustees athletics representative who had rolled over on the case of Terrell's eligibility months before. Lane told Gould that Skip Saal "should have not done this because it is a potential NCAA rule violation."

Lane said there "were two major issues in the last nine months and something needed to be done. I told him that he needed to get Bill Swan involved because I had no authority over the president and I could not stop him from putting the university in danger. I told him that I would be happy to talk to Mr. Swan to explain the situation.

"Later in the day, I again called Mr. Gould. He said that he had talked to Bill Swan and that Bill was contacting the president. Mr. Swan asked Mr. Gould if I was trying to hurt the president. Mr. Gould told him that he believed that I was not and that I was concerned about the university."

That same day Lane said he contacted Saal to tell him he's "just heard the day before that he allowed Jamil Terrell to withdraw from a class after the university appointed date upon the request of the president. I informed VP Saal that this was a possible NCAA violation and the athletic department did not request the president to ask for this change."

Bill Swan, the president's buddy, along with Gould finally decided an investigation was in order.

Chapter Fifteen

The whole issue was soon to explode and leave St. Bonaventure in national disgrace and a national laughing stock. Swan was too little, too late, to stop the situation from becoming both.

In testimony to the review committee, Swan said he felt Lane and Wickenheiser should have worked out the Terrell eligibility issue themselves. Remember that President Wickenheiser was "Bob" to Bill Swan, his buddy at ball games and Lane's boss. Swan reportedly told Gould, "This is something they have to handle and we can't get involved in it."

This is from a guy who carried a pocket card listing Franciscan values and flashed the card to others on occasion.

Swan apparently didn't want to get involved despite the possibility that his alma mater could become the subject of an NCAA investigation and penalties; despite the possibility that his school would become a national example of what's wrong with college sports when and if the role of the president in rule-breaking was revealed.

There was the need for action when Swan and Gould backed away from confronting Wickenheiser after he declared Terrell eligible despite Lane's warning.

But Swan, who was –remember—chairman of the university board of trustees, had told investigators in April of 2003 that his "own life was too complicated. I really don't have time to be involved."

He said that when he was first told about the eligibility question by Gould he "felt it was time to back off, and at that point I didn't want to call Bob, challenge his authority or our confidence in him." Swan said his reading of the email that Wickenheiser took as his own though it was written by his son, Kort, sounded "like he knew what he was talking about."

Bob Wickenheiser testified three times to investigators that spring, The first time he said he wrote the email. The second time around, he admitted his son had written it.

Lane says the university produced the email only after he identified it among all the documents sent to him by the NCAA as part of their investigation.

Prior to St. Bonaventure's appearance before the NCAA Committee on Infractions, the NCAA asked Lane for assistance in finding several emails that Lane knew existed and were pertinent to the investigation. SBU had previously refused to grant Lane access to his office computer or his email file.

The NCAA sent Lane a DVD of all emails to and from Robert Wickenheiser, Kort Wickenheiser, and Jan van Breda Kloff from SBU email system. Within fifteen minutes, Lane was able to find several key emails. Among those was the email exchange between Bob and Kort proving that Kort Wickenheiser did actually write the email Bob Wickenheiser used to respond to Gothard Lane's June 16, 2002 email challenging Bob's decision to declare Jamil Terrell eligible.

Lane told the author he found a copy of his May 8, 2002 email, that SBU said it could not find proving that Lane had emailed Bob Wickenheiser about Coastal Georgia's determination that Terrell's certificate in welding was not equivalent to an associate degree. For Terrell to be eligible right away, he needed to have an associate degree from CGCC.

Swan took another soft line with Bob Wickenheiser in February when he found out from Jim Gould that Terrell had been given an incomplete in Spanish 201 through a sweetheart deal. He called the president. "I got on the phone with Bob dealing with this supposed incomplete that was changed to a withdrawn on the record, and Bob challenged it, saying it had nothing to do with Jamil Terrell, but more with a policy change that was loosely administered before. But we didn't like the sound of that, so it was brought up on whether there ever was an eligibility problem. So because of us raising the question, Bob became uncomfortable and three days later he did the self-report," Swan said.

In his testimony Swan said Lane should have called the NCAA with his concerns about Terrell's eligibility. It seems a fair statement. The author asked Gothard Lane why he didn't blow the whistle to the NCAA himself on Wickenheiser. His responded that it was the president's responsibility to self report his transgression, that he (Lane) reported his concerns to the

Chairman of the Board of Trustees who decided to support the president ." I report to the president, and such as it goes in the armed services, the chain of command must be respected," he said.

Wickenheiser told the author that he was not going to offer Lane a new contract when his current one ran out, thus—in effect—firing him. Lane said he knew his situation, and so did Swan and Gould. Wickenheiser didn't like to be disagreed with, to say the least, and he had been undermining Lane's authority in athletics for nearly two years through son Kort and van Breda Kolff.

On one occasion, Lane told the internal committee, Bob Wickenheiser lost his temper completely when he felt challenged by anyone about his son. It was after a Bona defeat.

"We lost the game, Lane said (Steve) Mest said the players won't talk, and the whole world breaks loose. The next day, Thursday, he (Wickenheiser) calls and says come on over and have a meeting with you, Mest, Jan and Wade."

Jack McGinley: Whose decision was it- the athletes or the coaches?

"It came from Marques Green who had a tough interview after a brutal game. He got tough questions and he complained to Wade. He (Wickenheiser) calls us into the meeting and I thought we'd resolve it and he starts to rip Mest and I and blames us for it. I say wait a minute and I say to Wade, 'Mark did you not tell Steve this is what you wanted.' He admitted it but said, 'we shouldn't be getting the blame,' it should not fall back on the basketball staff. Wade said they were not supporting the program and I asked for an example, and right out of Jan's mouth, that Barb Questa was still trying to screw the program. Bob chimed in with the same thing, and then said that they certainly were not helping it. And then he said that you had no business talking to Jan about the academics."

"After the last away game, I was driving back to campus and I get a call from Steinke that there are four kids who are not eligible. Three had not registered yet and Jamil had three incompletes. When I got back, I got their input, and I waited for Jan and briefed him on this. I know that Kort knows this or maybe has told you, I told him. Jan said that Kort only tells him what he wants him to know. So at this meeting with Jan, Bob, Mark and I, Bob is lighting into me. He said that it was Kort's responsibility to talk to Jan about academics. He was wild; I thought he was going to die. He said I was a son of a bitch bastard. At that moment I left. Bob said to keep going and not come back. I immediately called Gould and briefed him. He wasn't just mad about the program, but the problem was that I told Jan something that was his son's responsibility. The anger in his face was something like I'd never seen before and it was a father protecting his son's turf."

Interestingly, Bill Swan said he couldn't "honestly remember " if he ever suggested to Lane that he contact the NCAA, or if he ever even discussed the possibility. Lane was all alone in his fight against the president. The basketball staff was at least partly against him, the two trustees that he had hoped would listen and act had walked away from him, and the president was a basketball junkie who made his own rules.

Hindsight always smoothes things over, so Swan had the chance to throw Bob Wickenheiser under the bus in his concluding testimony to the NCAA. "If anyone was corrupted here, and if you look at everything that has happened, Bob touched the eligibility. Bob touched the potential condoning of the players not playing. Bob is the central core here. There may be dysfunctionality (sic) and other things, but Bob is the key guy," Swan testified.

Swan was washing his hands of the president. But it was easy to do that after the national story had broken and Bona was publicly embarrassed and laughed at.

Lane had this take in 2011 on Swan's actions:

"He loved using his saying of "nose in, fingers out" with regard to why he was not more proactive with Wickenheiser after I asked him, Swan, for help. Once it blew up, and I had all of my emails between Wick and I, Swan had to explain why he was not more proactive with reigning in Wick. Not just with me but for years before. You know of all of the issues that the faculty had with him. Swan always backed Wick. So Swan had to throw him under the bus.

"Any organization involved in a scandal will protect itself first. That is what Swan did. Once it was clear that Wick had ignored my warnings, and I had the paper trail to prove it and that I had contacted the board and him, Swan had to protect himself."

Let's return to the narrative of what happened on the court and the end of Terrell's St. Bonaventure career.

Through early 2003 the men's basketball team, with Terrell playing regularly, had been having and off-again on-again season, and was in the midst of A-10 conference play.

It all came to an end on Feb. 24 when Lane said the president tried to tie the whole mess to Lane rather than himself. Lane said Wickenheiser "calls and tells me that he wanted to have the Atlantic 10 Conference rule on Jamil Terrell's eligibility and he asked me to send the conference office the appropriate documents. President Wickenheiser also stated that after he had informed Linda Bruno, Commissioner of the A-10, of this possible violation and that he told her that I had resigned.

" I immediately called Linda Bruno and told her that I had not resigned. I told her that I had no intention of resigning. I stated that I felt that President Wickenheiser was trying to link me to this possible violation by lying about me resigning my position. I also told her that we had a very detailed paper trail proving that the violation occurred in the president's office and not athletics."

The next day Wickenheiser called Lane into his office again, this time with a report that Commissioner Bruno would determine Terrell's eligibility. "At the end of this brief meeting, President Wickenheiser then handed me a letter from himself stating that he was not going to renew my contract as vice president for athletics," Lane said.

As is common practice, when Terrell's ineligibility was determined by the conference, the athletics department has prepared an NCAA form asking for the player's reinstatement, which included a detailed account of the violation. Gould saw that account and told interviewers when he then "finally" realized the magnitude of the issue.

The president, in the meantime, had called Linda Bruno, the A-10 commissioner, on Feb. 24 and told her he wanted her help in determining if the Terrell case amounted to an NCAA violation and a violation of conference rules.

Bruno told him shortly thereafter that it was a yes to both questions. He later testified that Bruno said Bona would forfeit its conference wins in the games Terrell played. Wickenheiser didn't pass this on to his athletics people.

Sure enough, on March 3, 2003, the Presidents Council of the A-10 ordered St. Bonaventure to forfeit six of its seven conference wins and barred the school from the upcoming A-10 tournament.

Wickenheiser was off on a trip to California at the time, meeting with a charitable foundation on a typical presidential mission to raise money. He was accompanied by Joe Flanagan, Bona director of alumni services.

When Wickenheiser received word of the A-10's actions, Lane says he didn't bother to tell him about it or the reaction of the team. In 2010, Lane recalled: "I did not find out about the player's decision to boycott until Steve Mest called me on the Wednesday morning of the day that the team was to leave Bona for their game against UMass. After finding out later that morning that the teams had a meeting the night before and that half of the team had already left campus on either Tuesday night or earlier Wednesday morning, I had a previously scheduled 12 noon conference call with Linda Bruno and the other A-10 ADs about the Jamil situation.

"I expected to brief Bruno and the other ADs that we may have a problem. As the call started and I told everyone about the potential boycott, Linda Bruno said that she already knew about it from the night before when she had talked to Bob on the phone after being tipped off by a Buffalo area reporter. I was furious. I asked her why she did not contact me on Tuesday evening either before or after talking to Bob (Wickenheiser) so I could have stopped the players. You always talk to the AD with regard to a team issue. If Bruno had called me, I could have prevented the players from leaving campus and the UMass game would have been played and that part of the scandal would have never happened.

"Bob also never called me on that Tuesday night to give me a heads up that he had talked to Kort and the team over the phone. Bob never even called George Solan that evening, (a university vice president) who was his campus problem solver with student issues.

"It is like both Bob and Linda wanted the situation to blow up. A phone call to me from either one of them on Tuesday evening would have put a stop to the boycott.

"Talk about having time to take the fuse out of a bomb before it blows up and no one bothers to tell you about the bomb!!

"In my humble opinion, Bob wanted it to blow up so he could fire both Jan and I and name Kort as the acting coach. If I remember right, Jan mentioned in one of his NCAA interviews that he felt that Bob wanted Kort to be the next head coach."

Chapter Sixteen

When the news media jumped onto the story at Bonaventure, first reports were merely about Terrell's ineligibility. But the actions of most of the players soon changed a decent story into the lead on ESPN's Sportscenter. It was the beginning of spring break on the Bona campus. Almost all the student body had left for home or for warmer climes.

But the men's basketball team had to stay and get ready for travel to play at the University of Massachusetts. What happened next kept Bonaventure on the front pages for days to come. Mo Young, a reserve forward and one of Terrell's apartment-mates, related the only inside look at the actions of the team:

"I can clearly remember that day as if it were yesterday. We had a Saturday afternoon road game at Temple University. When we returned to campus that Saturday night all the students had left for spring break. Coach van Breda Kolff gave us Sunday off from practice. Practice was scheduled for Monday at 10 am and our next game was Wednesday at the University of Massachusetts.

"I got to the Reilly Center an hour early to get dressed, taped, and to practice my shooting. When Coach van Breda Kolff came into the gym he looked confused. I was happy because I thought it was a sign that practice was going to be light or be cancelled. After everyone arrived, he called the team into the locker room for a team meeting and this is when he dropped the bomb on us.

"Coach began by telling us that he was not aware of all the details because he had just been informed about what had taken place 30 minutes before the meeting. He told us that Jamil Terrell had been ruled ineligible for competition for the remainder of the basketball season because the NCAA had questions about his transcript. Then he told us that we had to forfeit all the previous games Terrell had participated in.

"He proceeded to tell us that the A-10 had banned us from the 2002-2003 conference tournament. Finally he told us that the NCAA had barred us from playing in any post-season tournaments.

"After coach broke the news to us the room went into complete silence. Everyone was shocked and numbed because this news was totally unexpected. We had no idea that any of these penalties had been discussed. There were no rumors or anything that would have prepared the news that had been given to us. Coach instructed the players to go out the side doors because reporters were all over the Reilly Center and he did not want us to talk to the media.

"Most of the players went back to their rooms to try and digest this bombshell. I shared a town house with Jamil Terrell, Marques Green, Joe Shepard and Cortez Sutton, all members of the basketball team. We began talking about the things coach had said and we became, angry, frustrated and distraught.

"Terrell told us that he did not know his junior college education was invalid. He was just as shocked as we were. He was also angry and hurt. The more we talked the angrier we became.

"Most of the other players came to our room for direction, support, and answers. We called coach and told him to come to the townhouse because we needed to talk to him. He did not have any answers to our questions and he was evasive to most of our questions. He took a seat on the floor with his head in his hand as we talked, cursed and screamed about the situation. We told the coach to call President Robert Wickenheiser. Later someone was able to reach President Wickenheiser and a couple of players talked to him with no success.

"After several hours of ranting and raging over this matter, out of anger and frustration, the team voted not to play the last two games. This anger was directed more toward coach van Breda Kolff because we felt he was lying or hiding the truth from us. Coach was sitting on the floor when we made our decision and he never told the team that we had to play the games. We would have been upset but we would have played. The university was on spring break and there were not adults that we could talk to or seek advice and guidance from.

"A couple of players left Monday night. There were rumors that the DC Crew - Calvin, Amad, Cortez and myself - left first, but this is not true. I drove the four of us to the Buffalo airport on Tuesday morning to catch a flight to

Baltimore. When I got home, I received love and support from my family and friends once I explained the situation to them.

"My older brother Marcus, told me that what the team did was unprecedented and to expect backlash and negative comments. He was right. Once the media found out that we had decided not to play the last two games, all hell broke loose. ESPN, Fox Sports, USA Today, the New York Times and the Washington Post, and others made our controversy the lead story or headline.

"We had no idea the decision we made would receive national exposure and such harsh ramifications. The decision was heard everywhere around the sports world. SBU and Olean became famous because of the negative publicity and were discussed for over a month. All the national sports shows bashed the players and called us 'quitters.' The incident and imposed penalties shattered our post-season dreams and threw away all the hard work, commitment, dedication and sacrifice we had made through the season."

Lane as well as Wickenheiser, had been on the road when the A-10's actions were made public. Lane was at his Maryland home. He was getting ready to travel to the A-10 women's basketball tournament. He returned immediately to Olean on Tuesday and met with his staff. Once Steve Mest called Lane on Wednesday morning about the boycott, Lane met with the five remaining players who were still on campus including Marques Green. One of the five players was injured and could not play. Green refused to play and the other three did not know what they wanted to do.

Lane is bitter towards Bruno, who he says was eased out of her A-10 job in 2009, and also angry with the AD at Dayton.

"On late Wednesday afternoon the players realized that the world was falling in on them from everyone in the country for not playing the game against UMass," says Lane.

"They came to me and wanted to play Dayton as scheduled on Saturday. I called Ted Kissel, Dayton AD, to say that we would play the game and that we would even come to their place. I got him on the phone as he was leaving the office. I told him that we wanted to play the game and again, we would come to their arena if they wanted. Ted said, and I will never forget these words, 'No, we have moved on' and hung up.

"Just like Linda Bruno not contacting me after she and Wick talked on that Tuesday night so I could have a chance of holding the team together, it seems nobody in the A-10 wanted to help Bona in anyway. If Dayton would have played, that part of the scandal would not have been as bad."

Chapter Seventeen

The players had met and their decision to not play seemed to have been guided mostly by the leadership of Marques Green, the explosive point guard. Green was the player who called Wickenheiser in California to discuss the situation, believes Vinnie Pezzimenti, who was a basketball student manager at the time.

Green told SBU-TV, the campus tv newscast : "We understood we were going to forfeit all the games before that that Jamil played in. That wasn't the problem but when the A 10 said we couldn't play in the tournament, we felt real bad about that. We didn't understand. We wanted people to answer questions. The president wasn't here to answer questions for us so we kind of felt like where is everybody right now during this event? So as the day went on, we got, we learned that other people were involved with Jamil playing and things like that and we learned that some people that was involved and they was telling us they wasn't. So right then and there we felt betrayed a lot which we were and still to this day we feel we are.

"We want them (the public) to understand where we came from and just understand what we're going through. We're not just some spoiled kids that just 'okay we're not going to play.' It was a lot of things that went into our decision. And we just like I said we just felt disrespected and betrayed," Green said.

"Those were the guys who kind of kept everything together," said Pezzimenti, referring to Green and his roommates. "That was what was really missing because the seniors on that team, Robert Cheeks and Patricio Prado, weren't vocal guys so you know the guy at the top was ... Marques Green, and he wasn't necessarily the kind of guy who brought things together vocally…he was kind of on guys more than he should have been, instead of being encouraging as a leader should have been.

"It didn't sit well with certain guys on the team who were key players. I know Marques Green and Mike Gansey didn't get along and other guys too and there just was a lot of turmoil. There were obviously expectations that the team did not meet (on the court), specifically for that reason."

Pezzimenti said the dynamic of the team was one of dissention. "Just for example, Billy McCaffrey who was an assistant on that team, maybe showed some favoritism to Mike Gansey," he said. "You could see that kind of grated on someone like Marques Green. You could see he would show favoritism to a certain player and that kind of miffed him and you could see that. At one point, that kind of blew up in practice late in the season and there'd be a certain point when like Jan would see a practice wasn't going well, he'd (have) a two hour scheduled practice and forty-five minutes in he'd blow it up and that would be it and guys would be like just yelling at each other."

Pezzimenti is a journalism graduate of St. Bonaventure and currently works as a sports writer on an eastern newspaper. He is not a van Breda Kolff fan. "This is just my opinion, and probably other people hold this as well. I think that he was just kind of using this job. He wanted to get back to the East Coast so I don't think Bonaventure was the destination he wanted. He just didn't fit well. He was just using the Bonaventure job to get something bigger on the East Coast, the Big East or perhaps something along those lines.

"He just wanted to spend two or three years at St. Bonaventure and when things weren't going well he was really short-fused. This was his chance to move on and obviously he talked with people around the athletic department. He didn't fit in particularly well with those in that area."

Pezzimenti contends that van Breda Kolff's differences with Gothard Lane and others in the athletic department were partly a result of the coach's connections. "By having Kort Wickenheiser on his staff and having the president kind of in his pocket. I think gave him power over people in the department and he could make the decisions he wanted regardless of what was happening and who else had a say in it."

The former student manager said that van Breda Kolff openly talked about Terrell's eligibility issues the summer before the scandal season. "I remember being in the office after he (Terrell) had signed and van Breda Kolff and Kort talking: 'Do you think anybody's catching on about this welding degree?' 'Do you think it's a bad thing or what not?' At that point I didn't look too far into it. I figured he's got a welding degree but I figure every-thing's okay. That was my take on it," said Pezzimenti.

"The only thing I thought at that point was wondering how the public would perceive it, and things like that but as far as him being ineligible, I had no idea. I don't think anyone had any idea until it came out."

Chapter Eighteen

Bill Swan hadn't paid attention to Gothard Lane's calls for help about Wickenheiser's actions in declaring Jamil Terrell eligible. In fact, he had insisted that it was Wickenheiser's call and interference from the board of trustees was improper interference.

But on that Sunday, March 9, 2003, Swan acted with the support of the trustees. He canned Wickenheiser, and put Lane, Kort Wickenheiser and van Breda Kolff on administrative leave. The last three were told not to talk to the media about the scandal. Bob Wickenheiser was asked (told) to resign the presidency and he did so. University officials would not confirm a report that he was paid at least a year's salary.

The scandal had broken, and now Swan decided to jump in with all the CEO skills he had built up in his very successful banking career. He took a week off from his duties at the First Niagara Corp. and headed to Bonaventure. Two nights after the informal Reilly Center meeting that had attracted a few hundred, a majority of the student body of 2000 students made their way back to Reilly to hear Swan preach.

""We will not sacrifice our values for anything, not even athletic glory," Swan told the gathering, waving his Franciscan values pamphlet as he spoke. Dave Ferguson told USA Today that Swan "had to practice that speech three times before he could get through it without breaking down. It was the moment in his life that he just wanted to do the right thing."

The so-called "Unity Convocation" erupted in cheering when Swan said his "values" line, and many on hand left feeling much better about where they were working or going to school. It would sort of be an "us against the world" attitude among the administration for a long while, and students either vigorously defended their school choice to friends, or just put their Bonaventure apparel and gear in the back of their closets so they couldn't be identified as "welding school" when they went home on the next school break.

Lane feels the destruction of his career began that week. "I was in complete shock because Jim Gould called me on Saturday and said, 'Bill Swan and I have talked. You're okay. You did the right thing. I'm going to tell everybody. You're going to be safe. But we're probably going to do something with Bob.' When I got the call that Sunday evening saying I was on administrative leave, I almost fell off my chair," he said.

"The next day, I received a call from another trustee who said that they were sorry for what happened and that I was going to be ok until one major and very wealthy trustee who was a close friend of Wickenheiser demanded that if Bob was going to be let go that everybody was going to go."

"Also, about a week later, a prominent lawyer in Olean who was close to the SBU situation told me that it all came down to either Swan or I and that Swan was left standing because he had a bigger check book than I did."

"They put together a review committee and they put a gag order on me. I couldn't talk to the media. At that point everyone was saying, 'You're going to be okay. We're going to have this review committee review everything. You did the right thing.' I talked to (Sister) Margaret Carney and she said, 'We think you did the right thing.'" Lane said he could see when the review committee started it was going to take a long time. He didn't like the way it was looking. He could see that his days were numbered because they were kind of championing Barb Questa even though Questa had signed the "NCAA Squad List" which is "To Qualify student-athletes for intercollegiate competition and assess compliance with NCAA Financial Aid Rules."

SBU insisted that by Lane signing the "Student-Athlete Affirmation of Eligibility Form" that this allowed Jamil Terrell to play. During the NCAA's investigation of St. Bonaventure, the NCAA Division I Committee on Infractions requested a copy of the NCAA Squad List form from SBU. In fulfilling this request, the NCAA was sent an unsigned copy of the form. Once again, the Committee on Infractions contacted the university asking to see a signed copy of the squad list form. SBU sent the form, also signed by Questa.

To be clear, neither form put Jamil Terrell on the court. Bob Wickenheiser's decision to declare him eligible did that. The NCAA's Division I Committee on Infractions knew this and that's why neither Lane or Questa were charged with a violation.

The national media had treated St. Bonaventure's troubles as another outrageous example of big time college sports gone awry. This time, however, it was a college president in their crosshairs, instead of a coach or a bunch of players. Although the Bona players had done something that offended some columnists who were outraged they had refused to play their final two games.

But it <u>was</u> different. "This is no college basketball scandal out of central casting," wrote Ian O'Connor in USA Today. "On some level this is worse. This is a case of a blinded-by-the-lights college president overruling his compliance director and admitting a junior college ballplayer whose academic credentials –he had a certificate in welding—would scare off most street agents.

"This is a warning for every Iona and Manhattan out there, for every little guy fixing to play big...nothing devalues a degree quite like the moral sacrifices often made along the way."

New York Post columnist Mike Vaccarro is a St. Bonaventure alumnus. He was so upset that he wrote a column suggesting that other alumni join him in taking off their class rings.

Lane looks back today on the events with an interesting viewpoint. "With regard to Swan, he loved using his saying of 'nose in, fingers out' with regard to why he was not more proactive with Wickenheiser after I asked he, Swan, for help. Once it blew up, and I had all of my emails between Wick and I, Swan had to explain why he was not more proactive with reigning in Wick.

" Not just with me but for years before. You know of all of the issues that the faculty had with him. Swan always backed Wick. So Swan had to throw him under the bus. Also, by that time, I believe Swan knew that Wick's plan to force him off the board as he did with Les Quick. Wick had told me of his plan to do so before things blew up and I had mentioned it to Jim Gould. Gould may have told Swan."

Leslie Quick is a Buffalo banker and Bona alumnus who served early as a trustee in Wickenheiser's tenure. It is widely accepted on the Bona campus today that Wickeheiser did indeed force him off the board. But Lane's contention that Wickenheiser wanted his basketball buddy Swan off the board is surprising.

In that week following the break of the scandal, Bill Swan flexed his management muscle and convinced his fellow trustees to call for immediate formation of an internal committee to investigate the entire matter. Its members included fellow trustees: Ellen Grant Bishop and Col. Maureen Keenan LeBoeuf, Pittsburgh lawyer McGinley, plus ex-trustee Les Quick.

Also on board were Dr. Joseph Zimmer, chairman of the Bona faculty senate and a School of Education professor; Father Tom Blow, guardian of the Franciscan friary, and Brittany McVicker, president of student government. Swan also hired Hilliard, the Indianapolis lawyer, whose law firm Ice Miller, had dealt with the NCAA on violations matters regularly.

This committee began hearings within a month and invited several of the principals in the scandal to explain what they knew and what they didn't, what happened and who did it.

After the university interviews ended, a representative of the NCAA, Jeff Higgins, the assistant director of enforcement, called further hearings to investigate the whole mess from the point of view of the college athletics administrative body. St. Bonaventure had already done what is called "self enforcement, "when President Wickenheiser announced the forfeit of six wins in which Jamil Terrell had played.

The NCAA hearings began in June of 2003 and concluded in July. They were all held on the Bonaventure campus with Hilliard and Carrie McCaw of Ice Miller serving as counsel to the university and Higgins on the phone representing the NCAA. In late July, Tom Hosty, director of enforcement for the NCAA joined the group by phone for the second piece of testimony by President Wickenheiser.

The spring of 2003 was a stressful time to be an administrator at the university. Father Dominic was learning the ropes of the presidency, with Sister Margaret as one of his most trusted advisors. Admissions for the fall freshman class were pretty much completed, but there was nervousness among the admissions staff that many of those new students were cancel over the summer because of the scandal.

The university committee that had held its own interviews over the spring issued its own a report in mid April. The report found that St. Bonaventure had violated two major NCAA rules, and pinned the blame on Wickenheiser, van Breda Kolff and Gothard Lane. Even though Rich Hilliard had formerly been an NCAA enforcement official, he went along with the committee when its report cited two NCAA violations. Only the NCAA Division I Committee on Infractions has the authority to determine if an institution has violated NCAA rules so the SBU report was simply the university's opinion.

Van Breda Kolff immediately fought back. He and his lawyer, Lew Conner, scheduled press conferences on the same day in Buffalo and at Mickey Mantle's Manhattan restaurant in New York City, where the ex-coach expressed a lack of knowledge about Terrell's academic situation. This despite reports that he had discussed Terrell with President Wickenheiser and Lane, testimony from Kort Wickenheiser that he knew about the player's ineligibility. The same assertions came in an interview with the author from Pezzimenti, the student manager who said he witnessed van Breda Kolff and Kort Wickenheiser talking about the ineligibility in the summer of 2002.

An outraged ESPN columnist who also happens to be a Bonaventure journalism graduate, jumped on the ex-coach with both feet. Adrian Wojnarowski wrote: "Van Breda Kolff brought a lawyer, a swarm of public relations suits and a thick packet of irrelevant and irrational materials that didn't prove his innocence, just his arrogant belief that people are as stupid as he is morally bankrupt.

"Nobody told me," van Breda Kolff said, his nose growing longer than Mick's Louisville Slugger's on the wall. Somehow, he insisted he was completely ignorant that there was even an issue on his eligibility. He said he never had a meeting on it. Never had a conversation. For goodness sakes, even Nixon finally came clean."

Wojnarowski's cynicism was shared by others.

Barbara Questa, the assistant AD at Bona had earlier been replaced as the compliance officer by Lane to "save her job" in his words. Questa spoke out about van Breda Kolff. "It surprises me he would say that ('Nobody told me') since he was in a meeting with Gothard (Lane) and me, where we talked about this issue. I also know that, through Gothard, he had a meeting with the president and Gothard about it where it was discussed," she told ESPN.

"Asked whether van Breda Kolff pushed for St. Bonaventure to accept the welding certificate and declare him fit for a scholarship, Questa said, "He was certainly an advocate of making him eligible," Wojnarowski wrote.

Chapter Nineteen

During the final months of the semester, the team began to break apart. Gansey, who had two years of eligibility left, announced that he was transferring to West Virginia. He would play and star under Coach John Beilein, the same coach involved at Canisius several years before when Wickenheiser refused an offer to play in the "Big Four" at Buffalo's new downtown arena. Prado and Robert Cheeks graduated.

Terrell moved on to West Texas A & M, a Division Two college where he sat out a year. He played his last two years of college basketball there, and then went to New Zealand, where he signed with a professional team and was played in the Kiwi land in 2010, then moved to a club team in Turkey.

Marques Green would return to become the star of a woeful Bona team the next season. Van Breda Kolff became an assistant coach with the NBA New Orleans Hornets. Kort Wickenheiser hooked on over the summer as the head basketball coach at Holy Cross High School in New Orleans, where he also taught chemistry.

Lane had returned to his Maryland home and began a job search.

Meanwhile, in what was a rush to judgment, the Bonaventure Basketball Program Review Special Committee (a zenith in awkward titles) wrapped up its investigation in mid-April, 37 days after the trustees had forced Wickenheiser to resign. The witnesses during their interview sessions included van Breda Kolff, Mike Russell; his wife, Barbara Russell; Heather Jackson, who had succeeded Barbara Russell as university registrar; Barbara Questa; Skip Saal, Leigh Simone, Julie Steinke, Steve Mest, Gothard Lane, Kort Wickenheiser; Bob Wickenheiser; and finally Bill Swan.

The report to the trustees concluded that "The interviews and the evidence … can be relied upon to reveal an over-involved president preoccupied with the success of the men's basketball program; a men's basketball coaching staff in constant conflict, real or perceived, with athletic department administrators; and an SBU men's basketball program in turmoil."

The report also concluded the university was in violation of three NCAA regulations. Remember, this committee did not represent the NCAA nor would its findings be part of the NCAA report later on. In fact, the NCAA report was quite different than the one issued by the Bona internal committee.

Bill Swan, the chairman of the board of trustees, and the guy in charge of the committee's formation, strangely wasn't criticized in any way in the report. Or maybe it was not so strange, as he would have to take some of the blame if he was criticized for not listening to Gothard Lane.

In fact, the report said he was advised by Swan that (the president's actions) were "an internal issue." Swan was seemingly off the hook for not questioning his president about an issue that could (and did) blow up to a national disgrace.

In a backhanded way the report alluded to his lack of action by proposing a new standard:

"The Committee recommends an extension or redefinition of the grievance procedures, the roles of the Advocacy Officers, and/or the creation of an ombudsman position at the University. Current policies dictate that all complaint procedures at the University currently end up with the president for his or her disposition. The Committee recommends that the Governance Task Force of the University re-examine these policies and procedures with an eye toward placing a system of checks and balances on the power of the president in resolving disputes and alleged policy violations.

"The Committee recommends that a system be put in place where the Board of Trustees could be clearly alerted to serious compromises of the mission of the University outside of the chain of authority in cases where those compromises directly involve the established chain of authority."

The SBU report also targeted Gothard Lane. "The Committee finds that Lane made a determined effort to bring Terrell's ineligibility issue to the fore and avert the issue of being noncompliant. However, these efforts, laudable as they may have been, were then followed by his execution of the 2002-2003 NCAA Certification of Eligibility in October of 2002 for the men's basketball team, which included Terrell – a document that Questa refused to sign…While one may sympathize with the conditions under which Lane worked, he should not have signed the certificate."

The SBU report never made a mention of Barbara Questa signing the NCAA Squad List form.

That criticism refers to a document the NCAA requires from both the coach and the AD of a varsity team attesting to the eligibility of all the players on a team roster. Lane said he signed the document because Wickenheiser and Swan had both agreed that Terrell was eligible and "I had no where else to turn."

He was also said to have violated compliance policies at the university by taking Questa off the direct oversight of men's basketball and replacing her with Steve Campbell, even though Questa still reviewed men's basketball issues. He did this the season before when Wickenheiser ordered him to fire Questa and Steve Mest.

Lane told the author: "When the president was demanding that I fire her, I would bring her in and say, 'Look I'm trying to keep you out of trouble, you know. Try to watch how you deal with basketball.' At one point I said, 'Don't even walk over there. If you need to find anything from basketball, ask me or ask Steve Campbell to do it. Stay out of their line of fire so they don't keep pressuring me to get rid of you."

The committee report finding about Lane is somewhat foggy. It says: "Additionally, the Committee believes that the information used to support a finding of an NCAA violation also supports the fact that Lane failed to meet his job responsibilities, as described in the University's compliance Polices and Procedures, when he removed Questa from her compliance responsibilities with the men's basketball program. Specifically, section 1, page 5,- 6 -"Administration," where Lane's position (Athletics Director) is defined, states: "This person is accountable for the supervision of all personnel and ensuring compliance with University, Atlantic 10 and NCAA rules and regulations."

SBU alleged that by replacing Questa with Associate Athletics Director Steve Campbell as the daily contact with the basketball office (even though Lane did so in order to keep President Wickenheiser from firing Questa) Lane did not "adequately monitor the University's men's basketball coaching staff after he instructed Questa not to interact directly with members of that staff regarding compliance issues." The final NCAA Committee on Infractions report did not find Lane guilty of any violations.

The media received copies of the internal report and it was posted on the university's web site. It took Lane two and half years and a lawsuit to be fully vindicated. The report also commented on Skip Saal's involvement in allowing Terrell's withdrawal from his Spanish course after the normal deadline, and the role of Bob Wickenheiser and Kort Wickenheiser in the whole thing.

Saal, the report said, was called on January 5, 2003 by the president who related that his son Kort had told him about a misunderstanding about a student-athlete who had missed a deadline to withdraw from a course. "Saal recalls R. Wickenheiser stating that K. Wickenheiser had ensured the student-athlete that the withdrawal would be possible. Saal also reported that he felt uncomfortable being questioned by the president about the fairness of his decision to enforce a policy.

"When questioned about why he was uncomfortable, Saal elaborated that when he was interviewed he made it clear to the president that he did not want the position if the president would be heavily involved in the academic affairs decisions. Saal reported that R. Wickenheiser 'honored that request amazingly well' and that this request was a bit out of character for him.

"The obvious connection with his son made Saal uncomfortable, but he clearly stated that he made the decision to approve the withdrawal, in the best interests of the student involved. Saal has the authority to change grades. Saal agreed to the change after being persuaded that changing policy in mid-year could be unfair to students and after realizing that a similar change had been made that semester for a non-student-athlete.

" <u>Saal inquired of staff and was assured that this would not constitute an NCAA violation. There is evidence, however, that neither the professor nor the student-athlete were aware that the change had been made and that the change did, in fact, constitute special treatment.</u> (author's emphasis.)

Saal testified that he "received assurance from Questa and Steinke that changing the grade would not violate an NCAA rule. According to Barbara Questa's interview, Saal never met with Questa and Steinke until February 10, 2003. That was over a month after he changed the grade.

Gothard Lane takes exception to what Saal told the committee. Saal testified that he "received assurance from Questa and Steinke that changing the grade would not violate an NCAA rule. He never met with Questa and Steinke until February 10, 2003. That was over a month after he changed the grade," according to Lane.

As we found out in their testimony, Leigh Simone and Jamil Terrell told investigators that they were never told of the grade change before it happened. It seems Saal was covering his own rear by first testifying Wickenheiser didn't influence his decision, (which seems unlikely), and second, that there was consultation ahead of time with both the Athletic Department, the professor, and the student.

Saal later wrote a letter to committee chairman McGinley citing an email he received in December from Julie Steinke (the athletics academic advisor) which said Ms. Steinke had talked to Dr. Simone about the possibility of Terrell withdrawing. "She said she would do it to help him so that he doesn't have to face any serious repercussions for having a GPA (grade point average) below 2.0," he quoted Steinke as saying in her email.

What Saal doesn't say to McGinley is that he never talked to Steinke or Simone until after the fact. Changing a grade without talking to the professor is about as serious an academic transgression that an academic administrator can do. It corrupts a school's integrity and is a clear violation of rules at Bonaventure and probably every other college or university in the United States.

The internal investigation had only tagged four men in the end." The machinations were directed at a declaration of the individual's eligibility for Division 1 basketball. R. Wickenheiser, Lane, van Breda Kolff, and K. Wickenheiser knew or should have known that their conduct fell significantly below the values cherished by this institution," said the report.

"But their collective acts of commission and later omission did not end with the issue of eligibility. Within months, some of these same administrators and coaches persuaded, cajoled, and directed a faculty member and University administrator to bend and then break certain academic rules at SBU governing course withdrawals.

"The cost of these many transgressions has been enormous, not to be measured only in dollars and cents. Rather, the moral integrity of SBU has been compromised as has its reputation for the intellectual and ethical development of its student body. The restoration process shall be far more arduous than the shortcuts designed and implemented by those who held perceived success in college basketball above the University's Franciscan values."

On the Bonaventure campus the report hit home in several ways. Some faculty and administrators worried that the fall out of the scandal would cause a drop in enrollment. The university is tuition driven with a small endowment. A reduction in the average number of freshmen of as little as 50 a year would mean the loss of 50 pays over four years. Tuition, room, board and fees in 2003 totaled about $32,000. Do the math and you'll find a possible income drop of $6-million over four years. The reality at Bona is that students pay an average of around two-thirds of the previous number, or about $20,000 a year, what with scholarships and various forms of aid. Today they pay nearly $38,000 a year retail.

The 2003 number was still a reduction of about $4-million over four years for just one entering class.

When Robert Wickenheiser came aboard as president, the university was in tough financial straights. His leadership pulled the school up by its bootstraps, but his actions in the Terrell eligibility matter could destroy everything good that had happened under his watch.

Then there was the matter of alumni giving. Would graduates who had been giving stop or reduce their gifts because of the scandal? The new president—a friar who didn't even want the job—faced the worst problem in Bonaventure's history, the loss of its reputation as well as its necessary income.

Chapter Twenty

The internal university report was prepared by Rich Hilliard, the Ice Miller lawyer who had been hired by St. Bonaventure to ensure that its actions would square up with NCAA regulations. Hilliard had been with the NCAA working in compliance for many year, and had left to make his income dealing with schools in trouble with the NCAA.

Figuring out the arcane and complicated NCAA regulations is challenging, so Ice Miller had established itself as the home for ex-NCAA lawyers who could bring in millions helping colleges in trouble. In December 2003, seven months after the Bonaventure report was issued, Hilliard connected with another big client, the University of Missouri head basketball coach Quin Snyder.

According to records on file with the Illinois Attorney Registration and Disciplinary Commission, Hilliard took a $15,000 retainer fee check provided by Snyder and, rather than depositing it with his firm, used it to pay gambling debts. When Ice Miller found out, he tried to cover his tracks, going so far as to forge fake e-mails from Snyder indicating he hadn't paid the retainer.

Hilliard didn't deny the charge. While his Chicago attorney, James Joseph, said his client had no comment, in a filing with the disciplinary commission Hilliard admitted the charges and asked the Illinois Supreme Court to suspend his license for no more than five months. Hilliard admitted in the file that he has been receiving counseling for a gambling problem since August 2003, while he was working for SBU and four months before Snyder hired him.

Hilliard served his suspension and as late as 2008 was doing the same kind of work at Ice Miller. Two years later he was no longer listed on the law firm's web site.

The internal report had listed two major NCAA violations, obviously Hilliard's estimation, as he was the only one on the committee with knowledge of the regulations. Yet, the committee report had no authority to determine what NCAA rules had been broken. It was not in its purview.

On campus, Father Dominic assumed all the duties of the president, but he had some extra help. A Franciscan nun, Sister Margaret Carney, was already a vice president of the university, and was promoted to senior VP to give the quiet president extra support. Sister Margaret, a life-long sports fan, particularly of her home-town Pittsburgh Steelers and Penguins, was (and is) an enthusiastic supporter on Bonaventure athletics, including the high-profile men's basketball team.

Both of the administrators, the trustees and the student body had to wait several months for the NCAA report. What would it bring? First expected were added sanctions beyond the self-imposed forfeit of six games. Action by the A-10s booted Bona from its year-end tournament. But what else? Would the players move in boycotting the final two games result in even stiffer penalties? That didn't seem likely, as it wasn't an institutional action. However, the NCAA might use that as a mitigating factor when it slapped Bonaventure with punishment for the "crimes" of its administration.

Lane had been fired, as well as van Breda Kolff and Kort Wickenheiser. Lane was removed from his job though he was the one who had been protesting all along to his boss that the situation was a violation of NCAA rules and more importantly, just plain wrong on an ethical basis. He had signed the NCAA Affirmation of Eligibility Form, as Lane later said "the president declared him eligible and the Chairman of the Board of Trustees agreed...Either I sign it or I get fired and since Swan refused to help me control Wickenheiser, I also feared that Questa, Mest and Morel would be fired and the department would be in the hands of the basketball staff."

As Thomas Yeager, NCAA Division I Committee on Infractions Chairman said, "the individual that basically bore the responsibility for the violations that occurred here was the one who had the ultimate authority at the institution; that being the president that basically declared over the objections of the athletics director and his compliance staff that the young man was going to be certified eligible."

Lane had an interesting piece of testimony to the NCAA that might explain why Bill Swan didn't step in and save his job when the scandal broke;

when he was placed on administrative leave along with Kort Wickenheiser and van Breda Kolff.

In his testimony about the morning he found out Bona players were going to boycott, Lane called Bill Swan, who was on a skiing trip in Utah. "I yelled at him, and told him to get Bob the hell out of athletics...I'm screaming at Swan. There were no players left that we could even draft on campus. The last thing Swan said before he hung up was that he should have paid attention to me last year," Lane testified.

But Swan didn't talk that way when he gave an interview to the Rochester Democrat & Chronicle on March 12. "Lane first came to us in June and said this guy can't play for us," Swan told the newspaper. "But Bob (Wickenheiser) assured us everything was fine with Terrell's transfer. He quoted some NCAA precedents and it all sounded OK.

"We thought it was something they just had to work out. We had full confidence in our president. We trusted him. It wasn't our role to get involved in that situation."

Swan said Bonaventure is a university "embedded with Franciscan values. It's a special place... This could happen at any school. It's good people making dumb mistakes." He did criticize Bob Wickenheiser for allowing his son Kort to be hired as an assistant coach, saying that "in hindsight" it may not have been a good idea.

Lane wanted his job back when he testified on March 27th. He was angry: "And what have I gained from standing up for the university?" Lane said. "My contract was not renewed, my competence was attacked in the media for my assumed wrongful actions and inactions. And now I have a smeared reputation from one end of the country to the other.

"I have not made any comment defending myself, and I have been instructed not to say anything by the university. My silence has been interpreted my many that I have something to hide.

"I ask and need to be vindicated by the university, reinstated to my position and my contract renewed as soon as possible..." he said. "I tried to do the best I could in a bad situation."

Lane didn't get his job back. He was to suffer far more than the others who were guilty of violations in the end, yet he couldn't get the university to help him restore his reputation, let alone give him back his job. On the evening of April 14, 2003, Lane received a call from his attorney who told him that the university was going to terminate him the next day and release their internal report.

"The next morning I went over to Hopkins Hall, the SBU administration building, to try to meet with Bill Swan and fight for my job. Swan arrived at the building the same time that I did," Lane recalled. " He agreed to meet with me along with Jack McGinley and Father Dominic in the president's conference room. "

"I proceeded to tell them that I had six years in compliance experience at the University of Maryland and the results of their internal investigation were wrong. First of all, I told them that they did not have the authority to decide if any NCAA rules were violated. Only the NCAA Committee on Infraction had that authority. Secondly, I had not violated any NCAA rules or regulations. I begged them not to terminate me. I asked to stay on for a year and I would try to find another job. They told me that they had to meet with some of the local media and asked me to come back in two hours. I agreed.

"I continued the conversation for a short time with Father Dominic in the hallway outside the conference room and he said that they might be able to let me stay on for a year. I left and called a member of my staff to tell them that it was looking positive."

"When I came back in two hours, the mood of Swan, Monti and McGinley had changed dramatically. They told me immediately that it was too late to change the report even though Bill Swan mentioned the Richard Hilliard was still writing the report in another room down the hall. I asked them to take out my part in the report until the NCAA completed its own investigation. Again, the three of them refused to consider my plea saying that they had only an hour before the press conference and there was not enough time to make any changes in the report. I again reiterated that I did not violate any NCAA rules and they were going to destroy my reputation and career. The meeting then ended."

"Just four months later, on August 15, the NCAA proved that I was right and SBU, Swan, McGinley and Monte were wrong. The NCAA did not include me in any of the allegations of rule violations they levied against SBU. Had Swan, McGinley and Monte listened to me, they would have saved the university a great deal of embarrassment and years of protracted litigation and legal fees."

"When I think back to 2002-03, again no one wanted to listen to me about Jamil Terrell and President Wickenheiser. Chairman of the Board of Trustees Bill Swan wouldn't listen and rejected my warnings. I was the only person on campus willing to fight the president while trying to solicit help from the trustees to control the president. If either Wickenheiser or Swan had listened, the human tragedy of the scandal along with the public relations tsunami that damaged the national reputation of SBU would have been adverted."

The NCAA investigation followed the university's and it came up with radically different conclusions as far as Gothard Lane was concerned. It exonerated him completely, going so far as to send him a letter in September of 2003 that read: "The enforcement staff does not consider you 'at risk' in any of the alleged violations, and as a result, you are not required to respond to the Notice of Allegations, or appear before the NCAA Division 1 Committee of Infractions." The letter was signed by David Price, vice president for Enforcement Services of the NCAA. It showed a copy had been sent to Father Dominic, now in his sixth month of serving as Bonaventure's interim president.

Lane felt he had been vindicated by the NCAA by not being charged with any violations, but the university didn't respond that way. "I spent a lot of money on legal fees, trying to get the university to admit that they were wrong; that I had not violated any NCAA rules. And after two years and spending a lot of money, they finally settled with me.

"(But) they said in their own review report that I violated NCAA rules. And just four months later, the NCAA Notice of Allegations cleared me."

" I was not listed on the infractions I was not charged with anything. Four months before in April, the campus is saying I did violate rules and the NCAA said I didn't. So I went back to campus and said, 'Look, I want you to make a release saying you were wrong.'

"They would not do it....They sacrificed me and then they wouldn't admit they'd had been wrong. Finally, on February 6, 2006, almost three years after wrongfully accusing Lane of violating NCAA rules, SBU issued an apology to Lane. Unlike when it kept its April 15, 2003 report on its website for almost a year ever after the NCAA cleared Lane, SBU never posted the apology on its website or released it to the media.

The university's curt statement (no doubt lawyered to death) said:

"St. Bonaventure University acknowledges that, in the NCAA August 15, 2003 Notice of Allegations to the University, the NCAA Enforcement Staff did not identify former Vice President for Intercollegiate Athletics, Gothard Lane, to be an individual at risk in any of the alleged violations involved in its case. In addition, the University agrees that the NCAA Committee of Infraction did not make any findings or impose any penalties against Mr. Lane in it February 19, 2004 St. Bonaventure University Public Infractions Report.

Sr. Margaret Carney, O.S.F., President"

During that two-year period Lane said he tried to obtain 88 different jobs. The St. Bonaventure scandal hung over his efforts like a cloud, he said, as the university continued to stick to its original report that pinned some of the blame for the scandal on him.

"Everything was so painful to my wife, to my in-laws, " Lane said. "They talk about being Franciscan but they were not true to their own principles. They knew I tried to stop it and they were deliberately cruel and just tried to break me. So I don't know where the Franciscan values were."

Lane's wife, Mary Lou, is also bitter. She contends: "I realized what an impossible mess it was for Gothard. He warned Bob, Jim Gould and Bill Swan. He implored their help and was rebuffed. At that juncture he realized that what the president wanted the president got. It then became a matter of survival not only for Gothard but for the staff he shielded from the president.

"At worst they could have said Gothard 'you are a good guy caught in a bad situation but we feel we need to clean house.'

"That would have been bad enough. But they shunned him and cut him off. And yet, after the NCAA Committee on Infractions report SBU showed no hint of remorse for falsely accusing Gothard of violating NCAA regulations.

"Their arrogance and self - righteousness is positively sickening. Contrary to their supposed Franciscan values, they chose to publicly humiliate, vilify, and destroy Gothard. For what purpose I still do not understand. What I do understand is their hypocrisy and cruelness knows no depths. "

Mrs. Lane's reaction speaks to her concern for her husband, but also to a blind-as-brass-monkeys stand by the Bonaventure trustees.

The NCAA Committee on Infractions issued its report in February 2004. In part, it said:

"For a case that was so devastating in its consequence, its scope is strikingly narrow. It involved the academic eligibility of one basketball student athlete who transferred to St. Bonaventure in the fall of 2002 after attending a junior college for two years. The young man earned a certificate in welding which clearly did not meet the requirements that he be a junior college graduate with an associate degree in an academic or technical rather than a vocational degree.

"Specifically the student athlete completed 54 credits at the junior college the majority of which were in vocational subjects such as blueprint reading, metallurgy and of course welding. All courses were accepted by the university in the fulfillment of a degree in sociology, even subjects in which the student athlete earned a grade of "D". Since relatively few of these credits were directly applicable to a sociology degree, 39 credits or 72% were accepted as unspecified course electives.

"The university's Director of Athletics and other individuals responsible for NCAA compliance objected to the certification of the young man's eligibility stating in written emails to the former president, quote, "The junior college registrar has spoken. The student athlete's certificate in welding is not considered equivalent to an associate degree program."

"A month later the Director of Athletics again sent another email stating, "In my opinion, if we declare him eligible, we leave ourselves open to a possible NCAA violation. I do not believe that we can ignore their, the junior college, institutional stance without putting ourselves into possible jeopardy. I do not believe that we can declare him eligible without taking a major risk."

"He further recommended a petition to the NCAA for review of the status. The former president paid no heed to his advice. Preoccupied with the success of the men's basketball program, the president sided with the basketball coaching staff of which his son was a member. A basketball staff that was in constant conflict with the athletic administration and the former president definitely overruled the objections of his athletic director and the senior associate athletic director for compliance.

"Acting on the president's orders, the young man was certified eligible without ever asking the Atlantic 10 Conference or the NCAA to interpret the specific facts of this case. The president and the university has characterized his actions as quote 'errors of judgment', the committee of infractions concluded these actions were more than simply errors of judgment.

"First, there was evidence that the president sought to avoid information that undermined his conclusions that the student athlete was eligible, second, the president should not have sided with the interest of the coaching staff which his son was a member and also should have relied on the advice of his athletic director and should have contacted the Atlantic 10 Conference or NCAA for specific interpretation applicable to the facts of this case."

The Committee on Infractions had not only cleared Lane, but had praised him for his actions. Its report didn't mention actions or lack thereof from members of the Bonaventure board of trustees.

By that time, the report was almost an afterthought because of what happened to Bill Swan.

Chapter Twenty One

The Bonnies Bandwagon is an on-line chat site devoted to St. Bonaventure basketball. In truth, its main subject is Bona men's basketball. It began to operate under a student webmaster in 2001, and had passed through the control of several others since then.

Like many sports chat sites before it, the Bandwagon at first had trouble staying focused on its principal subject. There were days, and even weeks, when a posting on politics or some social phenomenon would spur dozens of messages and responses, each becoming more vitriolic and nastier than the one before.

Even in 2010, when St. Bonaventure alumnus and resident Buffalo loonie Carl Paladino was running for governor in New York, Bandwagon members couldn't resist a long topic string on his candidacy, a glut of messages that became more bizarre with each posting.

Chat sites don't always attract the most balanced of people. By their nature, they draw eccentrics to post items like iron filings to a magnet. Some are basketball junkies, who spend their time ferreting out possible Bonaventure recruits from web sites devoted to high school prospects. Others constantly evaluate the players on the current Bona roster, sometimes allotting them the talents of Zeus, and sometimes kissing them off as not up to Division One standards.

Still others are old grads, who spend their posts on reminiscences of their days on campus. The most irritating are the posters who are critical of the individuals that make up the rosters and the coaching staffs. They second-guess player abilities, motives and moral fiber with reckless abandon. They impugn motives to people they don't know at all.

Many of them are downright nasty, sometimes as vicious as most of the commentators on cable news. There have been times that the webmaster on the Bonnies Bandwagon has taken the extreme action of throwing these kind of posters off the web site.

In 2003 the Bandwagon was full of posters venting their spleens at Wickenheisers—father and son—at van Breda Kolff, and at Gothard Lane. When the news spread that Bill Swan had not interceded with the president after Lane told him about the Terrell case, posters began criticizing Swan.

Some of the posts were harsh, accusing him of betraying the university and destroying the basketball program. One of them read that every time Bill Swan "opens his mouth, he hangs himself." There is little subtlety in the postings on this genre of fan sites.

On Aug. 15, 2003, the NCAA had sent a Notice of Allegations to St. Bonaventure which outlined three major things the university had done wrong, including that it "failed to demonstrate adequate institutional control of its men's basketball program." The notice identified Bob Wickenheiser, van Breda Kolff and his coaching staff as the accused parties. Contrary to SBU's Basketball Review Committee's Report of April 15, 2003, former Vice President for for Athletics, Gothard Lane, was not charged with any violations by the NCAA.

In the July-August issue of Trusteeship Magazine, Swan had written about his role and the role of university trustees in matters such as the Bonaventure scandal. "I have asked myself countless times: Did I make the right decisions?" he wrote. "Considering the information I had, and balancing it with my general sense of the responsibilities of trustees, I can report that I am at peace with my decisions."

On August 20, shortly before 7 PM, Swan's wife, Ann, went into the basement of the couple's expensive suburban home to find her husband hanging from a rafter. There was a note on his body. "— I am so sorry for the pain I have caused St. Bonaventure University, my family, friends, my colleagues at First Niagara and my beloved wife, Ann."

Bill Swan

Swan's widow, Ann, recalled: "The week before Bill died, he said to me, 'Have you seen the Internet?' And I said, 'Yeah, the idiots are at it again,'" Ann Swan recalls. "Well, I went to bed one night during his wake with this Bandwagon posting in my head: 'Every time Bill Swan opens his mouth, he hangs himself.'" "I feel so guilty," she told USA Today. "Instead of making a crack about the Internet posts, I should've given him what he really needed — a hug."

Taking one's own life is not a rational decision. It's believed the will to live is the strongest element in the human psyche. Yet Swan, at 55, took his life in what apparently was a measured decision, penning his brief suicide note and expressing sorrow for the "pain" he caused St. Bonaventure. It was about as shocking as any executive suicide could be, not because successful businessmen don't commit suicide. They do, with frightening regularity.

It was because of his reason on the note. It was as if Bill Swan had found himself guilty of oversight he should have exercised when dealing with Bob Wickenheiser.

"The welding jokes, the barbs, the slanderous comments about the university devastated him," Ann Swan said. "Here's a guy who spent his whole life supporting St. Bonaventure, and in 24 hours, it's the laughingstock across the country. "Bill was annihilated," she said. "He went into a shell. ... He felt as if his morals, his values and his soul had been attacked."

Swan's life had been involved with St. Bonaventure from the day he enrolled after graduating from the now-closed Bishop Fallon High School in Buffalo. He was from modest means, his father a bus driver, and his mother a waitress. At Bona he joined the campus radio station and was a disc jockey there. Later he became the "Brown Indian," the walking, talking symbol of the university's nickname for its sports teams, a name that lasted until political correctness caused a change to the confusing "Bonnies" moniker.

The Brown Indian dressed in ersatz buckskins and a brown-and-white feathered war bonnet much better suited to western tribes than the Senecas who lived near campus. It was considered an honor to play the role, and Swan played it to the hilt, roaming the sidelines at the Reilly Center, exhorting his schoolmates to cheer louder. St. Bonaventure once had a Brown Indian Squaw, but that experiment didn't go over as well, and was dropped after a few years.

Swan was an imposing physical presence at 6-4 and 240 pounds, much bigger than any Indian in the Seneca tribe whose reservation lands nearly abutted the Bona campus. When he graduated, Swan joined FNG, then known as Lockport Savings Bank, in 1987 after 18 years with Buffalo-based M&T Bank. He became president and CEO of the newly-named First Niagara Financial Group in 1989.

Ironically, the night of his death, First Niagara officials contacted their Buffalo public relations agency to discuss what's called in the business—crisis communications. The head of the public relations firm was and is Bill Collins, a Bonaventure graduate with close ties to the university and now a trustee, and a basketball fan who had been following events closely since the scandal surfaced.

Father Dominic, the Franciscan interim president told the newspaper that "Bill plunged into everything 1,000%. Once he was convinced something was right, he had difficulty understanding how someone might see differently. This was the only blemish on his record.

"To me, Bill never stopped being the Brown Indian. His role was to get everybody revved up, behind the team, to boost the school. But, in this instance, even if 80% of the people agreed with his decision, there was a hard-core, 20% who weren't willing to let it go. And Bill thought, 'I guess I've failed.'"

Sister Margaret, who was Father Dominic's right hand man (sic) on campus, issued a statement about Swan. "Bill recognized that his Bona years formed him, enlarged his capacity and gave him friends and mentors that were unparalleled," she said. "Alma mater means loving mother. St. Bonaventure truly was Bill's second mother. It took him in a life direction."

Swan's death occurred a week before the university returned to classes in the fall semester of 2003. The basketball program was in limbo, with a new coach; woefully inexperienced Anthony Solomon, who'd been an assistant to Mike Brey at Notre Dame. Solomon soon revealed he was a nice guy, but not much of a coach. He had been only peripherally involved in on-court coaching at Notre Dame, serving more as a recruiter under Brey.

But he was about as clean as any college coach can be, with impeccable personal references. Solomon's chances of recruiting any quality players for his first season had long disappeared. Every high school basketball player who was a possible Division One recruit knew that Bonaventure was going to be hit hard by penalties from the NCAA. It wasn't a question of whether, but one of how severe those penalties would be.

Gansey was off to sit out a year at West Virginia. Marques Green was back, and he would be the centerpiece of the first post-van Breda Kolff team. Bona didn't have much else to play with, and Solomon seemed to have little control over his team. Wags in the small Reilly Center crowds swore that Solomon's wife called in strategy to him during timeouts. If she did, not much happened anyway, as the team suffered blowout loss after blowout loss.

Finally, in February 2004, the official NCAA penalties were announced on a teleconference with the media and university officials. The NCAA's penalties were: "(1), that the university shall be publicly reprimanded and censured and placed on three years probation from July 15, 2003, which is the date of their initial report to the NCAA. (2), the university shall be prohibited from participating in any post season competition at the conclusion of this season, the 2003-2004 year, in addition the university shall be precluded from using any of the preseason exemptions available to it during the

2004-2005 year. The committee also adopted the self-imposed reduction in scholarships of two, loss of two scholarships for 2003-04 year and one scholarship loss for 2004-2005 year. The committee also accepted the self-imposed penalty reduction in coaches permitted to recruit off campus as well as the reduction in official paid visits from 12 to 10 for a two year period which is also self-imposed by the institution."

Most schools caught in apparent NCAA violations impose penalties on themselves rather then waiting for the NCAA to lower the boom. They know that self-penalties usually are no worse than what they'd get from the governing body, and sometimes are a bit lighter. Bonaventure's actions in cutting scholarships and reducing coaches' recruitment visits as well as visits to campus by recruits were accepted by the NCAA without any additions.

The NCAA summarized the violations, which, as Lane described them, were all in the area of academic corruption rather than athletic. "There are three violations in this case," the report said. "The first involve the conditions and obligations of membership in that the university failed to properly certify the student athlete for practice and competition. A second violation involved an extra benefit of an impermissible academic arrangement when at the end of the fall 2002 semester and at the request of his son, the president intervened to have an institutional grading policy changed to the benefit of this same student athlete. And thirdly, the former president violated the principles of ethical conduct and institutional control in that he failed to exercise proper control of the men's basketball program. There is also a finding of institutional lack of institutional control."

The report was probably not a favorite read at Skip Saal's house. The highest academic officer in the university had contended he changed the grade in Terrell's Spanish 201 course because it was "consistent with my decision to delay strict enforcement of the withdrawal deadline policy." That "decision" had been made at the intervention of Bob Wickenheiser, no matter how many ways Saal tried to dance away from it. Saal stayed at the university until the fall of 2005, when he announced his retirement.

Chapter Twenty-Two

The story at St. Bonaventure seems to be a quaint artifact of college sports gone wrong.

Compared to the constant beat of scandals involving players and coaches that's gone on since the winter of 2003. Perhaps, it is. Football players at Auburn were passed through courses they never even took, with A's or B's. Disgrace follows Kentucky basketball coach John Calipari wherever he goes, with his recruiting prize in 2010 an 18-year-old Turkish bigman who played pro basketball in his country for three years.

Auburn pops up again as the team quarterback Cam Newton chose after transferring from Florida, with a possible shakedown of Mississippi State by his father, said to be more than a $180,000 arm.

Just down Route 86 from St. Bonaventure, the State University of New York at Binghamton went through one of the sleaziest episodes in recent college sports history. The school, under President Lois B. DeFleur, a college basketball player in her right, beefed up its men's basketball program almost overnight. The beef was tainted, with players better suited as thugs than as college students.

In 2001, over the objections of many faculty members, President DeFleur moved the school into Division One sports and the state built a $33-million basketball arena on campus. For six years the men's team struggled in the low rung America East Conference. That cost the first coach, Al Walker, his job; with Georgetown assistant Kevin Broadus hired to replace him.

Broadus took the team to an America East tournament championship and a bid to the NCAA March Madness. Binghamton lost in the first round, but Broadus' team was supposed to be just the beginning of a rising star in the school's basketball fortunes. It was more like a shooting star, as soon after six players were kicked off the team and out of school for a variety of offenses that ranged from drug possession to buying goods with a stolen debit card.

Joel Thirer also resigned as athletic director, and Broadus was placed on administrative leave in 2009. He eventually received a $1.2-million settlement from the university (New York State) for – in essence—recruiting thugs to the basketball team. Dr. DeFleur got out while she could, resigning, she said, because of marriage plans.

The list of college sports corruption goes on and on, with a seeming-new scandal every few months. There may be another case like St. Bonaventure out there, with a president who'll be caught manipulating the athletic program against rules and ethical standards, but it hasn't shown it face yet.

The St. Bonaventure story was a toxic mixture of a father's ambitions for his son, a coach who played deaf, dumb and blind to the things under his charge, and a university trustee who fell down on his job and– by his own word– died for his failure.

After the shock of what happened had settled over the St. Bonaventure campus, students, alumni and the administration did rally. They knew the men's basketball program was almost mortally injured. The hiring of Anthony Solomon as the head coach brought a cheerleader to the top job, not a first-rate Division One basketball coach. Solomon was hamstrung from the beginning. He inherited a team stripped of Mike Gansey and scholarships.

More importantly, Solomon faced a serious recruiting problem. Don't forget that the scandal was already a result of the Bona recruiting problem, getting quality Division One recruits to the campus. The school had chosen to join the original "Atlantic Eight" instead of the MAAC (Metro Atlantic Athletic Conference) that is home to almost every other small Catholic college in the northeast, including traditional rivals Canisius and Niagara.

The Atlantic Eight begat the current Atlantic Ten and the conference is a hybrid of large enrollment schools with healthy athletic budgets, plus two smaller universities in Bonaventure and Richmond. It's rated by most journalists as a so-called "mid major," but has aspirations to compete on the level of the Big East, with all the attendant television income that would mean. St. Bonaventure has the smallest athletic budget in the conference, by far. Bona is the only school located in the boondocks, with its bucolic 500-acre campus along the banks of the muddy Alleghany River.

There is little if the buzz that comes with going to college in Washington, Philadelphia or St. Louis for an African-American who grew up in an urban area. College basketball is dominated by African-American players, so the attractions of Allegany, New York, or the time-worn city of Olean east of campus, are of little interest to a city kid.

It wasn't so long ago that cattle grazed on the back edge of the Bona campus, and students once dragged a cow into a Bonaventure dormitory. The cow, by the way, allowed its self to be led up a flight of stairs, but refused to go back down, thereby causing the guilty student pranksters to be caught, and some serious cleanup work after she was finally extricated.

Anthony Solomon faced an impossible task, recruiting for a school that had been pushed to the periphery of Division One basketball for 35 years because of its size and the changing nature of the college basketball world. His teams were hardly competitive. They won a mere 24 games, and lost 88 in four seasons, despite an out-of-conference schedule dominated by teams that used to be patsies for Bonaventure.

It was during the Solomon reign that the university found itself in yet another grade situation. The best player during those four years was a 240-pound, 6-10 center, Paul Williams, from highly-rated St. Patrick's High School in New Jersey. Williams ended up struggling in a sociology course taught by a woman professor who was not yet tenured, and his academic advisor in the Athletic Department urged him to withdraw from the course.

There were accusations that Williams has been caught cheating by submitting a paper copied in part from another source, and the whole matter ended up in the Buffalo News, leaked by someone on campus who claimed they knew the whole situation. Williams was identified by name in the newspaper story, and that set off Sister Margaret Carney, who had been university president for just a short time.

The incident was just about the last thing St. Bonaventure needed three years after the scandal. Sister Margaret called a meeting of the entire faculty and staff late one afternoon in a university auditorium. She was furious, and said so.

The diminutive president needed no microphone that day, nearly yelling, as she chastised all present for the leak of Williams name to the press. She warned that she would personally track down anyone who "ever leaks" this kind of information in the future. The author was present, and was shocked when the president said, "if necessary, I will track you down to the ends of the earth" if another leak happens. She said the university does not "wash its dirty linen in public."

Many who walked out of the auditorium that day were incredulous that the university president would dress down her faculty as if they were fourth graders being disruptive in the cafeteria. The incident reflects the tension about the basketball program that existed then, and still exists to this day. With little money, a small enrollment, and an uninviting life situation for many recruits, Bonaventure still tries to be competitive in the Atlantic Ten.

The coach that succeeded Solomon, Mark Schmidt, has improved the basketball team, but not in any substantial way. In 2010, one of the first blue chip recruits in years changed his mind after committing and went off to prep school where he thus would be free of his Bonaventure obligation and free to sign on with a bigger and better school. Another did the same in the spring of 2011.

Schmidt may not have been the first choice as the coach when Solomon was fired. He had moderate success at Robert Morris, and is a dynamic career coach. But he faces the same issues Solomon faced. Schmidt did an interesting thing in 2010. He left two scholarships unfilled rather then take players who were academic bottom feeders. Unfortunately, St. Bonaventure often faces taking a player who is both marginal in talent and in academic achievement. This can kill, on and off the court.

Afterward

It's been 60 years of watching big time college basketball for the author, and nearly as long watching college football played at the highest level. The standard of excellence that makes up the best teams in both sports has risen with more and better coaching, better training, and better athletes.

I've watched most of the greats, players who are in the Basketball Hall of Fame, and in various other award emporiums in both sports.

The best players have been a joy to watch. Some of the coaches were less than a joy.

I am certain of one other thing: that the so-called "programs" at the football and basketball schools are nothing less than professional sports hiding under the guise of competition among "student-athletes."

Hypocrisy is too mild a word to describe the hundreds of situations where the football or basketball coach (or both) make more than the president of the university where they're employed. The University of Florida athletics program, with its $95-million annual budget is the most visible gargantuan. But it's merely one of the most visible of the schools that have cast their lot for professionalism in their "programs." Ohio State is even bigger at a reported $115-million for athletics a year.

It's not that I begrudge colleges and universities expending their dollars in pursuit of that nebulous nirvana of national ranking, the Final Four, The Big Dance, or the BCS bowl. It's strictly business, and college presidents who aren't hypocrites admit that big time sports brings attention and alumni dollars to their schools.

The Chronicle of Higher Education (sort of a trade paper for college types) ran a story recently that delineated how many college presidents of public institutions are afraid for their jobs if they try and control athletic programs in any way. It seems presidents of many state schools that are football factories feel they'd be fired if they interfered in the caste system that pays football coaches $2-million and the best professors on their faculty but a tenth of that figure.

State legislatures have been known to step in and step on a university president who even just bemoans the ascendency of the athletics program above all others at their school. One can get fired for complaining about the situation where Coach Billy Joe Bobby Bob has linemen who take a bevy of courses designed for their intellectual level:" Football 101" or "Team Sports 202."

So it's best go along whether you're an academic at South Carolina, a president at Iowa, or a dean at UCLA.

Some college administrators report their schools don't make any money to speak of off their gargantuan sports programs. They say the millions in income are just poured back into more salaries for coaches, bigger stadiums, more training facilities, and even the wretched excess of a private air fleet at the University of Florida.

I am not the first to propose the following, nor will I be the last. Nonetheless, I propose that because income-producing sports are played by income-producing athletes, these athletes are employees in all but name.

They should be employees, paid salaries and benefits under a scale set by collective bargaining. If a school wants to produce BCS football teams or Final Four basketball teams, the players should be paid, and represented by their own organization that can bargain with the NCAA. I am sure there are a sufficient number of sports agents and lawyers who'd be glad to pull together that new organization, arguably titled the National Association of Collegiate Athletes (NACA).

It could bargain for salary minimums etc., and that contract should include six years of free tuition, room, board, etc. for the athletes it represents, the ones good enough to play (ahem) income-producing sports.

Paid college athletes would thus have the opportunity—should they wish to take it—of obtaining a bachelor's and master's degree without cost. These athletes would only have eligibility for four consecutive years, but that would leave them with the chance to finish a bachelor's at minimum in those extra two years.

My premise is that most athletes playing income sports are too busy to be real students (there are some notable exceptions) and are driven by their coaches to take as light a schedule that's allowed, plus take the easiest courses they can; just enough to stay eligible.

There would be no more eligibility problems because the athletes would be school employees just like the people in the admissions department, housekeeping, maintenance and so on.

There would be no subterfuge or hypocrisy involving these athletes. They'd be paid to represent the school in the arenas of combat that produce millions in income each year. They'd be under contract, a collective bargaining agreement, for six years. Then they'd be on their own, with no college degree, or maybe even that master's.

I imagine there would be some schools who are on the edge of things now, schools like St. Bonaventure that are Division One wannabes.

They play in a basketball conference that has visions of grandeur. Would it be worth it to Bonaventure to pay players and give them six years of grants in aid? Perhaps not, as the school already runs its athletic programs at a loss. There's no reasons schools like Bonaventure couldn't form an entirely different kind of college sports association, either as a part of the NCAA or in some other guise.

Athletes not good enough to turn pro in college could still play collegiate sports, without athletic "scholarships" just as schools in Division Three are doing today. The playing field would be leveled for the St. Bonaventure's of this world. Grants-in-aid for jocks could be given for academic performance or financial need. The games would continue, the competition between full-time college students, not the so-called "scholar –athletes" that the NCAA brags about today. Those "scholar-athletes" come from teams in the sports that don't bring in income.

You could put all the scholar-athletes in D-1 basketball in one motel, two to a room.

That, indeed, is a cruel exaggeration. But it not that great an exaggeration. Because of the insane NCAA insistence that basketball players can't turn pro until they are a year beyond high school, there's a common practice among the best of these "scholar-athletes" that involves enrolling at a college and attending enough class the first semester to stay eligible, then dropping out of all second semester classes.

Why go to class when all you're waiting for is NBA draft? There's no need to do anything but play ball in the spring semester, because you won't be academically ineligible until the end of the basketball season.

Notre Dame has a great reputation among the schools that play football at the BCS level and basketball at the national tournament level. In the 1930's my late father-in-law was an undergraduate on an academic scholarship at the nation's leading Catholic university. He was assigned a varsity football player as his room mate, with the explicit understanding that he would do papers for the jock if he (my father-in-law) wanted to keep his academic scholarship.

That's three quarters of a century ago, and it seems things have only gotten worse.

Until colleges and universities decide to clean up sports they will be a disgrace.

Bob Wickenheiser was a cause, and he also was a symptom; a symptom of college basketball's principal failing: winning at nearly any cost.

Coda

When I was at St. Bonaventure as a student a half century ago, I lived next door in a dormitory to a scholarship basketball player, one whose name is a major part of the history of the sport at Bona. In the middle of his first semester, that student's grades came back, and they weren't good.

A Franciscan priest lived on each dormitory floor, and he was indeed "in loco parentis." In fact Father Eddie hovered over us all like a wraith in a brown robe. He really cared about his charges in Robinson Hall third floor, and he made sure he knew everyone's grades and their peculiar social habits.

When the basketball player's grades were sent to Father Eddie, he called in the freshman and told him that he was grounded. He wouldn't be able to leave campus even on weekends until he pulled his grades up. And Father Eddie meant it. He was just enforcing the rules on campus that applied to all students who were screwing up academically.

That freshman 50 years later would have laughed at the whole thing. If he was pro ready—for the NBA or overseas basketball—he could have stopped going to class and probably got away with it.

Fifty years ago that Bonaventure freshman was reminded that he would be out of school on his butt if he didn't begin to study harder. So he did bear down, and after graduation, some All-American recognition and a brief NBA career, he went on to a graduate degree and a successful career.

Because that's when college basketball wasn't a "program." It was just basketball.

12175304R00074

Made in the USA
Lexington, KY
28 November 2011